1970s Jazz Fusion

Forthcoming in the series:

Vaporwave by Kirk Walker Graves
Field Recordings by Marc Weidenbaum
Noise Music by Natalie Marlin
Bollywood by Shwetant Kumar
Neo-Soul by Matthew Allen
20th Century Ambient by Dusty Henry
Plunderphonics by Matthew Blackwell

1970s Jazz Fusion

Matthew Reed Baker

BLOOMSBURY ACADEMIC
NEW YORK • LONDON • OXFORD • NEW DELHI • SYDNEY

BLOOMSBURY ACADEMIC

Bloomsbury Publishing Inc, 1385 Broadway, New York, NY 10018, USA
Bloomsbury Publishing Plc, 50 Bedford Square, London, WC1B 3DP, UK
Bloomsbury Publishing Ireland, 29 Earlsfort Terrace, Dublin 2, D02 AY28, Ireland

BLOOMSBURY, BLOOMSBURY ACADEMIC and the Diana logo are
trademarks of Bloomsbury Publishing Plc

First published in the United States of America 2025

Copyright © Matthew Reed Baker, 2025

For legal purposes the Acknowledgments on p. vi constitute an extension of
this copyright page.

All rights reserved. No part of this publication may be: i) reproduced or
transmitted in any form, electronic or mechanical, including photocopying,
recording or by means of any information storage or retrieval system without
prior permission in writing from the publishers; or ii) used or reproduced in
any way for the training, development or operation of artificial intelligence
(AI) technologies, including generative AI technologies. The rights holders
expressly reserve this publication from the text and data mining exception as
per Article 4(3) of the Digital Single Market Directive (EU) 2019/790.

Bloomsbury Publishing Inc does not have any control over, or responsibility
for, any third-party websites referred to or in this book. All internet addresses
given in this book were correct at the time of going to press. The author and
publisher regret any inconvenience caused if addresses have changed or sites
have ceased to exist, but can accept no responsibility for any such changes.

Whilst every effort has been made to locate copyright holders the publishers
would be grateful to hear from any person(s) not here acknowledged.

Library of Congress Cataloging-in-Publication Data
Names: Baker, Matthew Reed, author.
Title: 1970s jazz fusion / Matthew Reed Baker.
Description: [1.] | New York : Bloomsbury Academic, 2025. | Series: Genre: a 33
1/3 series | Includes bibliographical references.
Identifiers: LCCN 2024036336 (print) | LCCN 2024036337 (ebook) |
ISBN 9798765119525 (paperback) | ISBN 9798765119532 (ebook) |
ISBN 9798765119549 (pdf)
Subjects: LCSH: Jazz-rock (Music)–History and criticism. | Jazz–1971-1980–
History and criticism. | Rock music–1971-1980–History and criticism.
Classification: LCC ML3506 .B33 2025 (print) | LCC ML3506 (ebook) |
DDC 781.66/17509047–dc23/eng/20240823
LC record available at https://lccn.loc.gov/2024036336
LC ebook record available at https://lccn.loc.gov/2024036337

ISBN: PB: 979-8-7651-1952-5
ePDF: 979-8-7651-1954-9
eBook: 979-8-7651-1953-2

Series: Genre: A 33 1/3 Series

Typeset by Deanta Global Publishing Services, Chennai, India
Printed and bound in the United States of America

For product safety related questions contact productsafety@bloomsbury.com.

To find out more about our authors and books visit www.bloomsbury.com and
sign up for our newsletters.

Contents

Acknowledgments vi

Prelude: Jazz Has Never Been Pure, a Strident Manifesto about the Past vii

1 **The Promethean Leader: Miles Davis** 1

2 **The Everchanging Supergroup: Weather Report** 17

3 **The Funky Scientist: Herbie Hancock** 35

4 **Three Loud Visionaries: Tony Williams, John McLaughlin, and Chick Corea** 53

5 **Ten Crossover Virtuosos: Freddie Hubbard, Donald Byrd, Patrice Rushen, George Benson, Grover Washington Jr., and More** 75

6 **Two Pioneering Record Labels: CTI and ECM** 95

7 **Ten Jazzbo Rockstars: Joni Mitchell, Earth, Wind & Fire, Frank Zappa, Santana, Steely Dan, and More** 107

Coda: Jazz Fusion Has Always Been Current, a Joyous Celebration to the Present Day 127

Ten Essential Tracks 137
Notes 139
Select Bibliography 153

Acknowledgments

To Clair, Giulia and Ian, for your love and support, and for listening to this music with me at dinner, in the car, or wherever

To my parents, Leonard and Donna, and my big sister, Liz, for raising me in a house full of music

To my high school and college friends, who explored so much of this music with me at a wonderfully impressionable age

To the good folks at 33 1/3, who welcomed me to write this book, and my editor Annie Zaleski, who made it better

To Miles, Herbie, and Joni, for first showing me the way

Prelude: Jazz Has Never Been Pure, a Strident Manifesto about the Past

"Fusion is all crap," growled a grumpy Joe Zawinul. The year was 1978, and his band, Weather Report, was riding high in the charts and selling out arenas, so he felt haughty enough to berate a hapless *Los Angeles Times* reporter. "What's fusion? Can you tell me what it is? I think most fusion music stinks and to be put in the fusion category is an insult. It's the writers who are putting us in this category because it's easy and there's no other place to put us."[1]

A brash musical pioneer, Zawinul was not the type to tolerate being pigeonholed, but you know a genre has a bad reputation when one of its prime movers disowns it, so any book about it has to face this challenge head-on.

Despite the sting of Zawinul's crotchety comments, his broader question is what lingers: What is jazz fusion anyway? He blamed the writers for creating the phrase as a catchall genre as if it were some big storage bin to stash musical odds and ends. And he's not entirely wrong. Jazz fusion is frustratingly vague, if just because nothing else will quite do. "Jazz-rock" is a common term, but it ignores how the music can be funky as hell. "Jazz-funk" also sounds good, as long as you plan to ignore the music that rocks hard. "Jazz-pop" certainly doesn't work when you're faced with the dense textures and abstract jams of electric Miles Davis. And none of these terms works well when the music can also incorporate Brazilian samba or psychedelic electronics or gospel or Motown or avant-garde classical like Stockhausen.

Yes, 1970s jazz fusion has swallowed elements of all these genres, and it has fused them into a dazzling array of musical alloys. But if there are any overall defining characteristics of an average jazz fusion release, they would most often include: the usage of rock riffs or funk grooves, or both; amplified electric and electronic instruments; a memorable melodic motif or bass ostinato, even if it's as brief as a few notes; and a bigger, brasher attitude that aimed for a larger audience beyond the safe intimacy of small jazz clubs. Of course, there are fusion albums and artists that still don't quite fit these criteria, but one thing that's always true is that you can find in 1970s jazz fusion some of the most thrilling, demanding, inspiring, and *fun* music in the history of jazz, despite the naysayers.

And the naysayers are plenty. The first jazz fusion records arrived in the late 1960s when jazz overall was struggling with sales. Just a few years before, young music fans could show off their Miles Davis records as a totem of cool, but by the middle of the decade, they turned to rock and R&B for the next hip thing. Miles and other jazz legends like Donald Byrd thought so too, and as they reached mass audiences with their new thing called fusion, they were quickly accused of selling out and contaminating jazz's rich history. Nevertheless, jazz fusion thrived in the 1970s, becoming the dominant genre in jazz and helping artists like Herbie Hancock and George Benson earn gold and platinum albums. Even with—or because of—this success, it was seen as a slick, commercial hybrid, and like so many musical hybrids, it is still often dismissed as a compromise that kills tradition rather than as an innovation that refreshes it.

Most notably, it's astonishing how fusion is ignored or dismissed in today's established jazz histories. When documentarian Ken Burns's nineteen-hour, ten-episode *Jazz* series was aired in 2001, any music made after 1961 was crammed dismissively into that final episode, with jazz fusion in particular being mentioned only as an aberration. Gary Giddins is one of America's greatest jazz writers, and yet when he released the masterful 700-page *Visions of Jazz: The First Century* in 1998, the only 1970s jazz fusion visionary who commanded his or her own chapter was Miles Davis. And when legendary book editor Robert Gottlieb compiled the fascinating 1,100-page compendium of writings called *Reading Jazz*, his only nod to jazz fusion was Stanley Crouch's evisceration of Miles Davis's fusion years. At times like these, it feels as if 1970s jazz fusion has been erased from the canon of jazz itself.

These jazz histories ignore the fact that fusion artists were as bold and brilliant as any jazz innovators. For example, when John McLaughlin and Mahavishnu Orchestra incorporated Indian music into 1970s jazz fusion, it had a different feel than Dizzy Gillespie's Cuban experiments in 1940s bebop, but both had the same thrilling urge to explore diverse cultures. The funk of Herbie Hancock and Patrice Rushen in 1970s jazz fusion got your body moving in ways that made you forget history, but so did Duke Ellington's big-band recordings of the 1930s. Jazz is notoriously hard to define, which explains why it's diced up into countless subgenres. In fact, you can trace its beauty back to its creation in nineteenth-century New Orleans, when African, Latin, Moorish, and European musical traditions converged in rhythm, melody, tone, and instrumentation.

In 1985, musician and educator Billy Taylor coined the phrase "Jazz is America's classical music" to highlight how this homegrown art form created by Black culture should be venerated as much as any European symphony or cantata.[2] It's a crucial argument for the artistic primacy of jazz, and yet the phrase itself has also long been used to overprotect the music as if it can only survive with purist gatekeepers as its curators. Witness Wynton Marsalis, the senior creative consultant on Ken Burns's *Jazz*: Back in the 1980s, Marsalis was an astonishing young trumpeter from a family of New Orleans jazz royalty, a Grammy-winning musician, and a daunting musical scholar who cofounded Jazz at Lincoln Center. His opinions carried weight, and if there's one thing that Marsalis always hated, it was the notion of this pristine music being simplified and degraded by filthy funk and raucous rock. "Jazz was something that had deep blues in it, swing, had a conception of virtuosity, had deeper levels of expression, had a spiritual connection," he told *Paper* magazine. "Fusion was more pop music with the trappings of jazz. Like a hairpiece, it looks like hair, but it's not. You know what I'm saying."[3]

Okay, now *that's* a great quote, especially when you consider how hilariously hirsute musicians were in the 1970s. But it's also too pat, too easily dismissive of any music that strays from a purist mindset. After all, drummer extraordinaire Tony Williams never abandoned his astonishing virtuosity when he played deafening jazz-rock, while Herbie Hancock's mesmerizing funkathon "Chameleon" certainly swings. And even if jazz fusion was popular music, who can claim that the artists behind it had no deep levels of expression or spiritual connection to the music? So much jazz fusion exists because the artists had a vision of jazz where they mixed in something new that they loved and that spoke to them, whether it was the joyous throb of funk or the healing discovery of Buddhism.

So whether jazz fusion is a hairpiece or not, it fits one of the defining terms of jazz from Taylor's original essay: jazz's "bold tradition of constantly emerging musical forms and directions." And as if to underline the point, Taylor specifically makes room for fusion artists like Mahavishnu Orchestra, Stanley Jordan, and Paquito D'Rivera in that tradition.[4] Decades later in 2022, jazz-funk virtuoso keyboardist Patrice Rushen would phrase the same idea, even more elegantly: "Jazz is supposed to be a progressive music. It is supposed to allow for new ways to manipulate the musical language and elevate the landscape."[5]

*****

This book is a journey into this kaleidoscopic corner of jazz history. Hundreds of jazz fusion records were released in the 1970s, so any volume attempting to tackle it all is incomplete, but this one shall attempt a fair overview of the genre's main themes and artists. The biggest names are here, such as Weather Report, Herbie Hancock and John McLaughlin, and it all starts with Miles Davis, who may not have invented jazz fusion, but who did more than anyone to launch it as a phenomenon. However, these titans won't crowd out lesser-known but fascinating trailblazers, such as jazz-funk flautist Bobbi Humphrey and Norwegian jazz-rock guitarist Terje Rypdal. Any exploration of 1970s jazz fusion would be empty without the likes of Chuck Mangione and Grover Washington Jr., who scored huge pop hits—and perhaps are the key targets of Marsalis's "hairpiece" jibe—but also made jazz an everyday pleasure and gave it an everyday relevance again in the culture of the day. As will be seen in the lush, soulful recordings of CTI Records and the artful vigor of the German label ECM, certain record labels also played a large role in advancing this music, whether as commerce or as art. Lastly, this book will also explore how musical influences flowed in both directions, thanks to jazz fusion, as 1970s rock and funk icons like Joni Mitchell, Steely Dan, and Earth, Wind & Fire admired jazz and adapted it for themselves.

This book is not, however, a work of musicology, so it will take a different approach from most jazz books. For one, I am not a musicologist; rather I am a longtime arts journalist who has been a fan of this music since childhood. My mother went to college with Herbie Hancock, so she would tell me about him and proudly play his famous "Watermelon Man" on the piano. Then as a teenager, I put Miles Davis's *Bitches Brew* on a turntable for the first time, and my life was never the same. These musicians were brilliant human beings—many of them childhood prodigies—and it's a great pleasure to listen to their albums, write their stories, and show the impact they had on the cultural context around them. Their work is described less in terms of music theory and more in terms of how the music sounds, the images it evokes, and how it can make the listener *feel*. Even when 1970s jazz fusion reached the highest levels of intellectual concepts, it still managed to have a direct emotional and synesthetic effect on listeners. When this music hits the highest heights of invention, exploration, and groove, it feels like a miracle.

Even Weather Report's Joe Zawinul could feel it too when he was creating it. He fused eclectic genres under the aegis of jazz, reveling in new electronics and becoming a longtime devotee of R&B. "I do feel that we're coming from jazz, that the music is inventive and very powerful rhythmically, which is what jazz is all about," a more sanguine Zawinul told the *New York Times* in 1982. "The difference between what we do and what you might call straight-ahead jazz is, first, our rhythmic ideas are coming from everywhere, from all over the world, and second, that the energy of the rock age has affected us very positively." But he still didn't know what to call it: "As far as categorizing our music, I am always lost for an answer."[6] In these pages, we're calling it 1970s jazz fusion, and we're going to do it proud.

1 The Promethean Leader
Miles Davis

Even before the needle drops on the record, you already know from the album cover that the Miles Davis album *Bitches Brew* will be different from anything you've ever heard before. On many of his previous albums released in the 1950s and 1960s, the cover art radiated fashionable cool, thanks to their portraits of the immaculately tailored trumpeter himself or of his strikingly beautiful girlfriends, like actress Cicely Tyson. But when this double album *Bitches Brew* hit record stores at the end of March 1970, it splashed the shelves with a startling cover by a German-born painter named Mati Klarwein. Embracing the psychedelic vibes of the times, but with a hard-edged statement of Black identity, the gatefold incorporates a bare-chested African couple on the front, embracing as their hair and bodies merge with the storm clouds and the ocean. On the back, a high priestess in multicolored robes glares defiantly at the record buyer, as two hands—one Black, one White—intertwine. Whereas the earlier records went down nicely with a dry martini, you can easily imagine a grooved-out hippie grabbing *Bitches Brew* on that long-ago new-release day, then kicking back with this platter on the hi-fi, joint in hand.

Then the music starts. The first track is called "Pharaoh's Dance," and it begins with a shuffling but insistent rhythm that gives way to a murky, eerie soundworld. Three electric pianos drift around each other between the left and right speakers, as a bass clarinet and electric guitar slink around in the background like night creatures, while two bassists and four percussionists maintain an insistent pulse. It sounds improvisational like jazz but has the instrumentation of rock music, a groove as fierce as anything by James Brown, and the spacy haze of the best psychedelia. The song is an indulgent twenty minutes long, taking up all of side one, and Miles himself doesn't even enter the fray until two and a half minutes in, with a piercing cry far removed from the elegantly reserved tones of his earlier years. The music smolders with a blue flame for minutes at a time, then bursts into fiery cacophonies that burn out as quickly as they flare up. All of it is bathed in reverb that makes it sound like a transmission from a deeply funky field station at musical ground zero.

"[T]his is new and right now it has the edge of newness and that snapping fire you sense when you go out there from the spaceship where nobody has ever been before," wrote Ralph J. Gleason in the album's breathless lowercase liner notes.[1] Gleason was both a noted jazz critic and the cofounder of rock magazine *Rolling Stone*, so he was the ideal writer to herald this new music that bridged both worlds.

To be honest, however, other artists—some of whom appear later in this book—got there first, dabbling with rock energy and jazz chops in 1960s London and New York clubs. Even more, *Bitches Brew* was not the first at anything, not even the first jazz fusion double album. But it was the first to grab hold of both the jazz world *and* the mainstream. And that's not just because of the immersive power of its music, but because of the pervasive role Miles Davis long had in pop culture.

At the time he was going out there on that spaceship, he was the most famous jazz musician in the world, one who had the cachet of celebrity but also one who had earned artistic veneration as a lifelong innovator. No other artist had been part of so many of jazz's changes, from bebop in the 1940s to cool jazz and hard bop in the 1950s. And now that jazz fusion was entering the 1970s, his weighty imprimatur legitimized this new genre both artistically and commercially, inspiring whole generations of musicians and listeners to follow the path led by his light. So even if Miles didn't start jazz fusion, this book must start with him.

*****

Born in 1926, Miles Dewey Davis III grew up in East Saint Louis, Illinois, just across the Mississippi River from the great jazz cradle St. Louis. The son of a dentist, Miles was solidly upper-middle-class, growing up in a house with a maid and cook. He ended up being a 1950s and 1960s style icon, with his array of sports cars and sharp suits, and it all began with his father, who favored tailored waistcoats, and his mother, who wore furs and bespoke hats.[2] His father soon moved into a rural community, where he was one of the first Blacks to live there, a community that did not like non-Whites driving luxury cars and engaging in local politics, so he weathered threatening phone calls and stones thrown at the house as evening fell.[3] Miles never forgot this lesson from his childhood: No matter his financial comfort or cultural status, he could still be treated as poorly as any Black person in America.

Thankfully, starting at age nine, he also learned to play the trumpet. Miles played in his school bands and with friends. As a teenager, Miles auditioned on stage with the veteran jazz musicians passing through St. Louis and became a regular fill-in trumpeter for swing groups and jazz combos around Missouri. He was also invited to attend the prestigious Juilliard School, which was ready to train him to be one of the finest classical musicians in the world. But the school was also in New York City, the reigning jazz capital of the world. The year was 1944, and Miles arrived as bebop was shattering and reconstructing jazz with its lightning-fast, small-combo style that soon made the swing era a sepia-toned memory. Juilliard ended up being a dead-end blip in Miles's biography. Instead, he hit the legendary clubs in midtown Manhattan and thus began the most astonishing half-century of any musician in jazz history.

Countless books have been written about the details of Miles's career, and it's nearly impossible to single out even a mere handful of his achievements. First, Miles not only immersed himself in the highest levels of jazz but also played alongside the father of bebop, Charlie Parker, joining the band as a replacement for Dizzy Gillespie. By the end of the 1940s, he recorded a series of sessions with a nonet of jazz musicians, arranged by Gil Evans, and the brief tunes were all icy-smooth and airy—behold, "cool jazz" was born. The style dominated much of the 1950s, but Miles had already moved on, joining bandleaders like Art Blakey and Horace Silver in ushering in the hard-bop era, where R&B grooves leavened the virtuosity of bebop.

Miles formed his first great quintet in this era, with pianist Red Garland, bassist Paul Chambers, drummer Philly Joe Jones, and a young sax player named John Coltrane. But Miles never stopped moving, recording *Kind of Blue* in 1959 with a different band, exploring and popularizing "modal jazz," a more abstract style wherein soloists can improvise over musical modes that are much broader than the usual chord changes. It became one of the best-selling and revered albums in jazz history. Combined with his further explorations of orchestral jazz with Gil Evans—best exemplified in *Sketches of Spain* and *Porgy and Bess*—Miles was locked in as one of the most innovative jazz musicians, and also one of the most popular. After all, no one could match his charisma: He was strikingly handsome, dressed in elegant suits, dated beautiful women, and drove Ferraris.

By 1965, the Sixties revolution was ramping up, and after changing music four or five times, Miles formed his second great quintet: Herbie Hancock on piano, Wayne Shorter on sax, Ron Carter on bass, and Tony Williams on drums. Each of these five players had a brilliant mind in and out of music, and as a result, the musicians created cerebral albums that simmered with passion. Live, they pulled apart jazz standards and originals, reconstructing them at different tempos and exploring the limits of music without fear of failure. Once again, Miles was leading jazz into new realms of sound and ideas, and he was doing it all with acoustic instruments.

Davis recorded six studio albums with this quintet, all of them milestones in new approaches to composition—largely thanks to the genius of Shorter's pen—and improvisation. But the final two albums with this quintet signaled Miles's next drastic musical sea change: moving into jazz fusion. *Miles in the Sky* (1968), for example, boasted a track called "Paraphernalia," which featured George Benson as a guest on electric guitar—a first for Miles, even if Benson largely plays straightforward jazz with minimal distortion. Much more surprising is the leadoff track, "Stuff," which brims over with the funky swagger of Williams's drums, but also has Hancock playing electric piano on the record, which was hardly his idea.

"I walked into the studio and there was no piano for me to play," Hancock wrote. "At first I didn't say anything, figuring someone would take care of that little oversight. When that didn't happen, I finally said, 'Miles, what am I supposed to play?'"

"'Play that,' he said, and nodded toward the Fender Rhodes electric piano in the corner."

At the time, Hancock explained, the "conventional attitude" of jazz musicians was that electric pianos were insubstantial, lacking the full, rich sound of an acoustic. But Miles didn't care about conventional attitudes. Instead, he cared about throwing his bandmates into sink-or-swim conditions to avoid complacency. Hancock was skeptical but was soon won over not just by the pretty sonics of the keyboard, but because he could crank up the volume and compete with those powerhouse rhythms of Williams.[4] The word "pretty" barely conveys the effect of the crepuscular tones of the Fender Rhodes: a sense of luminous mystery hovers over the music like twilight, creating a mood that is so distinctive of jazz fusion in the coming years. It also was featured prominently in Davis's next album, *Filles de Kilimanjaro* (1969), which continued this progression toward electricity, grooves, and the looming influence of rock. The dreamy blues ballad "Mademoiselle Mabry" even quotes the first notes of Jimi Hendrix's "The Wind Cries Mary."[5]

Ever the seeker of new sounds, Miles was intrigued by saxophonist Charles Lloyd's group, who had gained fame at the Monterey Jazz Festival in 1966 by playing jazz with youthful rock energy. At the same time, he immersed himself in recordings by James Brown, Sly and the Family Stone, and especially Jimi Hendrix, whom he befriended. Miles could tell the music was changing fast, and he couldn't wait to form a new extended band to help him explore it.[6] And so, released in the summer of 1969, with a set of mostly new musicians, *In a Silent Way* was his first complete advance into electric jazz. Side one's eighteen-minute track, "Shhh/Peaceful," opens with just a sustained chord on electric organ, before flowing smoothly into a swirl of keyboards played by three masters who would dominate jazz over the next decade: Hancock and Chick Corea on electric pianos, and Joe Zawinul on organ. Even if Miles said that he only used future Mahavishnu Orchestra founder John McLaughlin for "special effects,"[7] the guitarist's licks are crucial because they firmly root this music in rock. Miles soars with celestial trumpet, Shorter searches on sax, and everyone rides cresting waves of hi-hat shimmer played by Williams, who holds the ethereal music in a suspended tension that never quite breaks. On the flip side, the twenty-minute side two track is a mash-up of the delicate ballad "In a Silent Way" and the funky jam "It's About That Time," anchored by Dave Holland's mesmerizing bass riffs. Other artists—especially in the UK—may have merged jazz and rock before Miles, but this beatific classic would have a quietly seismic effect, kicking off jazz fusion as a genre, because it was the first by such a musical titan.

Miles was accused ever after of selling out by giving way to rock, and to a degree he admitted to it. By 1969, "jazz music seemed to be withering on the vine, in record and live performances," Miles wrote. "It was the first time in a long time that I didn't sell out crowds everywhere I played ... Compared to what my records used to sell, when you put them beside what Bob Dylan or Sly Stone sold, it was no contest."[8] At this time, Columbia Records head Clive Davis encouraged Miles in this direction, and the trumpeter started bringing his vibrant new sound to the hippest rock clubs like the Fillmore East. Even more, those who revered Miles as a sharp-dressed style connoisseur were dismayed by his transition into counterculture clothing, but Miles saw it as a way to change with the times and as a way to outwardly express his identity: "Everybody was into Blackness, you know, the Black consciousness movement, and so a lot of African dashikis and Indian fabrics were being worn ... I had moved away from the cool Brooks Brothers look and into this other thing, which for me was more what was happening with the times." He even shopped at the same store as his friend Jimi Hendrix.[9]

If *In a Silent Way* was a tremor of radical change, then *Bitches Brew* (1970) was the earthquake. Where *In a Silent Way* was meditative and dreamlike, *Bitches Brew* was turbulent and loud—a roiling stew of rumbling polyrhythms over which Miles extended solos over clashing keyboards and stabs of guitar. He replaced most attempts at memorable melody with brief motifs, which were then repeated over widescreen tracks that can last almost a half hour long. So what was this music? To many critics and listeners at the time, it was so idiosyncratic and so uncompromising that one could just call it his own subgenre: "electric Miles." Either way, Miles would never again release another album of acoustic or conventional jazz.

Bitches Brew was a paradigm shift both in musical styles and in how the record industry perceived jazz. This dense, menacing double LP initially sold some 500,000 copies—or about 100 times more than one of his saxophonist Wayne Shorter's 1960 solo albums on Blue Note[10]—and was Miles's first album to go platinum.[11] His record company, Columbia, was thrilled, and so were rock fans who saw him opening for acts like the Grateful Dead or taking center stage at the Isle of Wight Festival. Though he was from an earlier generation, he had the intense aura of a younger star, and his new direction in music was bankable.

Miles's pioneering contribution to 1970s jazz fusion lasted only another five years. For the remainder of the decade, he retreated from music and society, sequestering himself in his house in a dark haze of drugs and depression. But from 1970 to 1975, the world was graced with so much "electric Miles" that it was hard to process it all. During this period, he released thirteen albums, ten of them doubles. Some were edited documents of live concerts, while others were spliced symphonies conjured from jams. By Miles's count, he went into the studio some fifteen times,[12] gathering more and more source material. Still other albums were a collage of live and studio recordings, featuring music edited together from different sessions and even from different years. Critics and fans felt challenged by listening to this relentless sonic mountain of molten lava, but Miles set their opinions aside; he was just trying to keep up with himself.[13]

For starters, the *Bitches Brew* era felt longer than it was, thanks to live albums. The first to appear was *At Fillmore*, a highly edited document of a four-night June 1970 stand at New York's Fillmore East. Then there is *Black Beauty*, recorded at San Francisco's Fillmore West on April 10, 1970, but only released in Japan in 1973. Here you have a complete performance of continuous music—with each of the four sides named just "Black Beauty Part 1," and so on—and you can hear Miles play fragments of recognizable tunes in order to cue the musicians to play in the next mode. But for the best sound quality, listeners had to wait until 2001 for the release of *Live at the Fillmore East (March 7, 1970): It's About That Time*, a concert that must have crushed the craniums of music fans who came to the club that night to see the other headliners, the Steve Miller Band and Neil Young & Crazy Horse.[14] As critics Richard Cook and Brian Morton write, "A genuinely important release, the Fillmore East gig is one of those rare occasions where one can hear the course of a genre change direction during the course of a concert."[15]

As he progressed into the 1970s, the albums focused entirely on rhythm and electronic modulation of energy and sound. Nonstop tracks filled whole album sides, and deep basslines made the music throb relentlessly—most often thanks to a young Michael Henderson, who came over from Stevie Wonder's band and served as a four-string musical metronome. But unique albums still emerged from this hyperthermic caldera of music. *A Tribute to Jack Johnson* (1971) is the closest Miles got to recognizable rock, thanks to searing guitar from McLaughlin and free jazz virtuoso Sonny Sharrock. *Live-Evil* (1972) was challenging to digest, a massive pastiche of December 1970 live sessions from Washington, DC's Cellar Door club; dry, hard funk from the studio; and drifting, ethereal snippets of an unfinished collaboration with Brazilian composer Hermeto Pascoal. Equally confusing but just as fascinating is *Big Fun* (1974), a neglected wonder where Miles and producer Teo Macero threw together music recorded between 1969 and 1972, editing it into four tracks ranging from twenty-one to twenty-eight minutes apiece. From spooky sitars to searing guitars to dusty funk, it flows like a river. It's easy to lose track of time in this music.

And then there's *On the Corner* (1972), the most controversial album Miles ever released. Inspired by listening to Sly and the Family Stone's hit album *Fresh*, he yearned to reach younger Black music fans. He invited a host of musicians into a darkened studio, where the tape just rolled on, recording rhythms and solos and sounds without beginning or end or defined takes. Again, Macero cut and spliced this river of sound, and the result was oppressively dense, with drum kits competing with tablas and handclaps, with more than a dozen musicians pulsing endlessly like infernal machines. Adding to the disorientation, Miles used a wah-wah pedal on his trumpet, and Macero boosted this distorting effect on the tapes and decided to "wah-wah them to death," as he put it.[16]

The album cover itself also drew controversy, as it featured colorful, cartoonish depictions of Black street life by artist Corky McCoy that seemed vulgar to jazz aficionados who were used to cool, stylized photos. Even worse, Columbia had zero idea how to market the record, using such cringe-worthy copy in magazine articles like, "Listen to music that captures the joy, the pain, the beauty of people who live on 'The Block.'"[17] And once they heard the music inside, critics derided it as "repetitious crap" and "an insult to the intellect of the people."[18] Though Miles was angry and disappointed that this bold album was considered a failure, *On the Corner* has since been reappraised as one of his most influential albums—not so much for jazz, but as a template for hip-hop and throbbing, looping electronic music like drum 'n' bass.

Miles's influence on electronica would continue with his final and most magisterial studio album of the 1970s. *Get Up with It* (1974) was created from another hodgepodge of sessions over four years. The half hour standout track "He Loved Him Madly" is a haunting elegy to the recently deceased Duke Ellington, but Miles eschews any big-band feeling and opts instead for a static haze of haunting sound as if an organ is playing drones in a cathedral while plaintive solos and muted drums drift along. It's stunningly beautiful and sad, and if jazz fusion engendered ambient electronic music, it did so here; none other than Brian Eno has called it one of his major influences.[19] The other epic, "Calypso Frelimo," is a much more vibrant piece, and Miles named it in honor of the Frente de Libertação de Moçambique, who were then fighting for that country's independence. Even with its playful root melody, it also floats in space, and samples of it have been the source material for hip-hop artists and electronic artists like the Orb, who featured it prominently more than twenty years later on the album *Orbvs Terrarvm*.[20]

Miles closed out his 1970s output with four double live albums, each one boasting just four uninterrupted slabs of group funk improvisation. He plays relatively little on these albums—another cause for critics to dismiss them at the time—but instead, he's conducting these swarms of sound played by bands as large as nine musicians. Unfortunately, too many of these musicians are unjustly unheralded due to the relative obscurity of these albums. The relentless energy and power of this music owe so much to talented artists such as the bedrock of Michael Henderson on bass; Dave Liebman and Sonny Fortune on fiery sax and lyrical flute; Al Foster holding it all together on drums; guitarists Reggie Lucas and especially Pete Cosey, who filtered and distorted rock and funk maelstroms into avant-garde sheets of sound; and whirlwind percussionist Mtume, who gained mainstream success on his own without Davis, in the early 1980s with the R&B smash "Juicy Fruit."

Just as the studio albums were often composed through editing, these live performances were "composed" with a hand gesture, a nod of the head, or even a look from his penetrating eyes. *In Concert* (1973), recorded at New York's Philharmonic Hall, sounds like an adjunct to *On the Corner*—even boasting another Corky McCoy cartoon street-life cover—but without the pristine studio production, the muddled mix of live musicians takes away from what is otherwise mind-melting music. Much better is *Dark Magus*, recorded at Carnegie Hall in 1974, but only released in Japan three years later. As ferocious and intimidating as its album title, it's the most hardcore of Miles's electric albums, as his screaming organ and trumpet compete with three guitarists to see who can shred the loudest. Best of all, Miles recorded both his afternoon and evening concerts at Osaka Festival Hall in Japan on February 1, 1975.

Agharta and *Pangaea* (both 1975) bring all these elements of "electric Miles" together: Drums, guitars, and electronics swirl through periods of funk and rock, before exploding like supernovas and drifting into the cosmos. As Mtume put it, "Our concerts began like a balloon that was incredibly compressed. After that it was a matter of gradually letting the air out. The energy it took us to play at that level was enormous."[21]

It ended up being too enormous for Miles because he was gone for the rest of the decade. Even when he was recording such passionate and radical music, his body and mind were breaking down. For example, one reason why his trumpet playing sounds more pinched and ragged than cool and commanding on albums like *On the Corner* is that he had developed walking pneumonia.[22] He had hip problems, for which he overmedicated himself with pills, and he was a prodigious cocaine user. So he became a recluse for five years, sequestering himself in his house for long periods of time, living with debilitating drug and sex addictions, and becoming estranged from his family. "When my old friends came by to see how I was living they would be shocked," Miles reflected in his memoir. "But they didn't say nothing because I think they were afraid if they had, I would just put them out, which I would have."[23] It was a shockingly hard fall for this proud man, and many thought at the time that he had changed music for the last time.

And perhaps he had. By the time he was "tired of being fucked up all the time"[24] and returned to recording and performing in the 1980s, his music was no longer as challenging, but more user-friendly. Still electric as ever, the grooves and production were slicker, and he even recorded pop tunes like a cover of Cyndi Lauper's "Time After Time," which certainly helped him sell more records. He reentered the outside world as an omnipresent cultural icon: playing with his band on the TV comedy show *Saturday Night Live*, portraying a pimp on the hit cop show *Miami Vice*, and attending a high-profile dinner at the White House. Miles died at age sixty-five on September 28, 1991, from a combination of pneumonia, stroke, and respiratory failure,[25] and while he didn't change music one final time in his final decade, that's okay. He had done more than enough.

In the years since his death, the musical value of this short but prolific "electric Miles" era remains the subject of debate. By the 1990s, Stanley Crouch was one of the most famous and vitriolic detractors, who called the whole phase "progressively trendy and dismal" and bemoaned Miles's "pernicious effect on the music scene,"[26] a claim echoed by the *New York Times*'s Peter Watrous, who called it "the Miles Davis curse."[27] Critic Gary Giddins was much more circumspect: "Despite the contempt they provoked, these works are accruing esteem and will continue to be examined for what they convey about the potential for blending acoustic and electronic instrumentation, free form and song form, jazz improvisation and multiple rhythms."[28] And as time continues to pass, these forbidding albums have increasingly been reclaimed as a bedrock influence by artists as varied as Aphex Twin, Radiohead, Flying Lotus, and Joni Mitchell, who would later record with some of Miles's former sidemen.

But Miles's biggest sphere of influence is the group of sidemen who joined him on this electric revolution, like Herbie Hancock, Wayne Shorter, Tony Williams, Joe Zawinul,

Chick Corea, and so on. Ironically, while Miles's music became less commercial with each release, these erstwhile bandmates became bigger stars than ever in the 1970s, thanks to their own explorations of jazz fusion. Reading the credits on so many albums of this decade is an exercise in repeating famous names and recognizing connections, as so many of these musicians who cut their teeth on Miles's power cords would soon change the music on their own. And no matter how much they blazed through the 1970s, they always acknowledged Miles as the smoldering source, igniting them with his blue flame.

Ten Essential 1970s Jazz Fusion Albums by the Promethean Leader

- *In a Silent Way* (1969)
- *Bitches Brew* (1970)
- *A Tribute to Jack Johnson* (1971)
- *Live-Evil* (1972)
- *On the Corner* (1972)
- *Big Fun* (1974)
- *Get Up with It* (1974)
- *Agharta* (1975)
- *Pangaea* (1975)
- *Live at the Fillmore East—March 7, 1970: It's About That Time* (2001)

2 The Everchanging Supergroup
Weather Report

"Man, I am a pop musician and a jazz musician," Joe Zawinul told the magazine *DownBeat* in 1978. "I think jazz music is great because it is the music with the most spark and the most freshness. I think jazz is the pop music of the future."[1]

Zawinul had a reputation for making cocky statements, but at this time in his career, he had ample reason to make this bold proclamation. As the cofounder and keyboardist of Weather Report, he and the band were still riding high on their smash album *Heavy Weather* (1977), which boasted that unicorn of the jazz world, a big single with heavy rotation on the radio. "Birdland" was a six-minute suite that captured all of jazz history, filtered through a fusion lens, with orchestral sounds of big-band horns played by Zawinul on an Oberheim polyphonic synthesizer.[2] What made it pop was its super-catchy melody and dynamic energy; any listener even today can understand why it became the big hit. Thanks to "Birdland," *Heavy Weather* was on its way to going gold, selling more than 500,000 copies,[3] and reaching No. 30 on the Billboard 200 chart.[4] Weather Report had taken jazz from smoky clubs and staid conservatories all the way into the heart of the mainstream.

Bold hype was nothing new for Weather Report. Music fans and the press had closely watched and followed the band's every move since the group formed in 1970. Thanks to their years working with Miles Davis, where the bandleader and his bandmates pushed each other to expand jazz and launch fusion as a popular genre, Weather Report had instant supergroup status. Shorter and Zawinul had taken parallel routes to get to this point. Though he later branched out with a notable solo career on Blue Note, Shorter rose in stature as the saxophonist in Davis's Second Great Quintet. Zawinul, meanwhile, was an Austrian keyboardist who had studied as a youth at the Vienna Conservatory before coming to the States and serving as a talented pianist for legends like singer Dinah Washington. The musicians had met each other as relative unknowns in Maynard Ferguson's big band earlier that decade, and when Shorter was gaining fame with Miles, Zawinul was gaining fame with sax legend Cannonball Adderley. By the end of the 1960s, they became renowned as jazz fusion pioneers together in Miles's band, recording the jazz fusion landmarks *In a Silent Way* and *Bitches Brew*.

Zawinul and Shorter were standout composers. Enigmatic Shorter tunes like "Footprints" had graced Davis's albums all through the 1960s, while Zawinul became a vital composer for Adderley, penning the pop and soul crossover hit "Mercy, Mercy, Mercy" for the sanguine saxophonist. With Miles, Zawinul wrote not only the leadoff track on *Bitches Brew*, "Pharoah's Dance," but also the title track of *In a Silent Way*. Zawinul included his own version of "In a Silent Way" on his self-titled 1971 solo album, which continued the progression of Miles's eerie, floating fusion, much like Shorter did with his 1969 solo album *Super Nova*. While neither Zawinul nor Shorter played on each other's solo albums at this time, they both employed a Czech bass virtuoso by the name of Miroslav Vitouš, who had briefly played in Miles's live band in 1968[5] and had released his own adventurous solo albums at the end of the 1960s. By the end of 1970, the three artists decided to create a band together, choosing a name while brainstorming about what people do every day: watching the weather report on the evening news.[6]

Even at this earliest point in the band's life, the Weather Report jazz supergroup was really just Joe Zawinul and Wayne Shorter, plus the musicians they chose for each album to keep progressing with their sound. These two men both mined deep veins of genius, but as personalities, they couldn't have been more different. Zawinul was the tough-talking, tough-acting, dominant leader of the band, one who was unafraid to demand his collaborators follow his vision or get lost, one who was a voluble talker who was prone to calling himself "the baddest motherfucker on the planet."[7] Shorter, on the other hand, was a science-fiction nerd who once embraced the nickname "Mr. Weird" in high school, one whose inscrutable digressions made conversations with him delightful, fascinating, and confusing to collaborators and journalists alike. During the 1970s, he began practicing Nichiren Buddhism, which only seemed to fit a deep-thinking man who already spoke in Zen-like koans. As writer and Weather Report friend Hal Miller told music journalist Michelle Mercer,

> It was perfect because Joe was domineering and liked to take control anyhow . . . So he'd be fussing with the road crew and

Wayne would be standing by with a beatific, benign smile. I remember once I asked Wayne for the time. He started talking to me about the cosmos and how time is relative. Joe came over and said, "You don't ask Wayne shit like that. It's 7:06 p.m."[8]

Despite their differences, they had a telepathic understanding of each other and complemented one another both as musicians and as people. The spontaneous Zawinul composed his tunes through hours of improvising at home until he hit something that he liked, whereupon he'd complete the rest in a matter of minutes.[9] In contrast, Shorter—who earned a degree in music education from New York University—handwrote long, brilliant compositions on staff paper, sometimes as long as twenty or thirty pages. And yet he would trust Zawinul to cut this symphony-level writing down to manageable, accessible material,[10] which is ironic, considering how Zawinul kvetched for decades about how *his* earlier compositions for Miles had been slashed by the great trumpeter. Even at their most pyrotechnic concerts, the highlight was always the intimate moment when the two would improvise as just a duo, vamping freely on Zawinul's famous tune for Miles, "In a Silent Way."

But these geniuses still needed to fill out the band, so for their self-titled debut (1971), they added drummer Alphonse Mouzon and Brazilian percussionist Airto Moreira. Almost immediately, though, Weather Report's rhythm section was a revolving door, cycling musicians in and out, while Zawinul and Shorter changed the sound of the band, almost with every album. And in each case, they pushed the boundary of what jazz could be, a lesson learned from the mercurial Miles Davis.

"The six years I was with Miles, we never talked about music, we never had a rehearsal," Shorter told Laura Sullivan on National Public Radio in 2013. "Jazz shouldn't have any mandates. Jazz is not supposed to be something that's required to *sound like jazz*. For me, the word 'jazz' means, 'I dare you.' The effort to break out of something is worth more than getting an A in syncopation."[11]

And indeed, with *Weather Report* and its follow-up *I Sing the Body Electric* (1972), Weather Report broke from the strictures of straight-ahead jazz, while sounding like an extension of Miles's mind-expanding electric and electronic jazz odysseys. The first album positively shimmered with crepuscular, ethereal jams à la *In a Silent Way*, with Zawinul's spooky Rhodes electric piano and the rumbling rhythm section creating shifting grooves underneath Shorter's leads. Vitouš even made the jazz-rock vibe more explicit by adding disorienting electronics, such as using a wah-wah pedal while playing his acoustic bass with a bow.[12] As a whole, the debut was lovely in its vagueness, finding a tender balance between the bold and the diffident. Robert Christgau, the *Village Voice*'s self-styled "Dean of American Rock Critics," noted the heavy influence of Miles, identifying the intangible allure of the *Weather Report* album as "*In a Silent Way* played for atmosphere" and praising how "the tone-poem impressionism of side one does its mysterious work."[13]

But if *Weather Report* evoked the eerie calm of the seminal Miles album *In a Silent Way*, *I Sing the Body Electric* channeled the riotous turbulence of *Bitches Brew*. Here the tunes didn't float or soar but tumbled and snarled. The second side of this sophomore release was live, taken from a concert at Tokyo's Shibuya Kokaido Hall, and it revealed Weather Report as an uncompromising unit that flirted with the edge of cacophony while playing over hurtling rhythms that still transmitted a forceful pulse. It was fiery and not a little bit forbidding, and as per Shorter's later words, it did not sound like jazz. If anything, it was more reminiscent of intense, experimental rock bands like King Crimson and Soft Machine. However you heard it, whatever genre it eluded, it was definitely the sound of genius musicians saying to each other, "I dare you."

The irony is that even as the musicians were stretching the boundaries of what jazz could be, Zawinul felt that Weather Report had reached the limit of exploring this style. For their third album, *Sweetnighter* (1973), the band consciously started its transition to Zawinul's vision of pop musicianship. "I felt at that time, 'Okay, now this is enough we have done now, swinging around now, looking for each other, looking for things, very nice musically, but I want to now put in more of this rhythm and blues feeling,'" he explained in 1993. "By that time, I'd been playing eleven, twelve years in America, with some of the greatest people. So we decided to put on this tune 'Boogie Woogie Waltz'. For that beat, I wanted to have a funk drummer, it was only for the record."[14] Jazz drummer Eric Gravatt excelled on the complex *I Sing The Body Electric*, but now he was replaced by a Louisianian named Herschel Dwellingham, who had grown up idolizing Ray Charles, B. B. King, and Allen Toussaint.[15] Though Dwellingham lasted only this one album, his booty-shaking swing on ten-minute-plus grooves like "Boogie Woogie Waltz" and the positively filthy funk of "125th Street Congress" set the standard that Weather Report used for the rest of their career. It says much about this change of approach that *Sweetnighter* marks the earliest of many Weather Report records that hip-hop and electronic artists later mined for samples. In this case you can hear traces of it in music by DJ Shadow, Organized Konfusion, Aphex Twin, and most notably the Pharcyde, who used "125th Street Congress" in their 1992 hit "Passin' Me By."[16]

What *Sweetnighter* also signaled was the end of Vitouš's tenure with the band. A brilliant composer and passionate player, Vitouš wasn't down 'n' dirty on the bass. To get that sound on the record, Zawinul brought in Stevie Wonder's bassist Andrew White to augment the funk. Vitouš's last appearance on record with the group was on merely two tracks of what would be their first undisputed classic, 1974's *Mysterious Traveller*. The split was not pretty. The avant-garde Vitouš not only didn't have the feel for the new direction of the band, but he also resented it, using the harshest of terms with Michelle Mercer in *Footprints*, her biography of Wayne Shorter: "Number one, I couldn't play the Black funk, and number two, I was not supposed to. I am an innovator and a pioneer and an advanced musician, and I am right on the edge of developing new music. How can you put me in a Black funk band trying to make some money? It's not me."[17] Though he was a fellow conservatory-trained European, Zawinul disregarded accusations of "selling out." Ever since he was a teenager and a budding jazz musician, he had been evangelical about the beauty and power of R&B in America; after all, he had enjoyed his first hit years ago with Cannonball Adderley by incorporating it into jazz. If Vitouš didn't want to play it, he was out. Philly native Alphonso Johnson was in.

Even with this turmoil, *Mysterious Traveller* works as one of Weather Report's most brilliant and defining albums because the band walks a thrilling tightrope between the extended jams of *Sweetnighter* and the delirious space-jazz of the first two studio records. You can have the seismic grooves of "Nubian Sundance" and "Cucumber Slumber," the latter of which was built entirely around a colossal bassline that Johnson brought into the studio. But you can also have the mysterious abstraction of the title track and "American Tango," the latter being Vitouš's one composition on the album. As on previous records, Zawinul created a rhythm guitar sound by running his Rhodes electric piano through a wah-wah pedal, but now he added synthesizers, particularly the ARP 2600,[18] which brought the alien cosmos to the earthiest rhythms. Shorter played some of his most lyrical melodies and improvisations on his delicate tune "Blackthorn Rose," but also some of his most cryptic and unpredictable ones on the monumental title track, which bristles with menacing volume and angular melody. The whole sprawling journey ends with the ghostly, percussive reveries of "Jungle Book." To this listener, more than any Weather Report album before or since, *Mysterious Traveller* combines the sequencing and cohesiveness of the best progressive rock albums, but meshed with a soulfulness that frees your ass along with your mind.

After *Mysterious Traveller*, Weather Report found a bit of stability with their sound, even as band membership continued to be in flux. For *Tale Spinnin'* in 1975, Leon "Ndugu" Chancler manned the drum chair; he had played in Santana, as well as acclaimed fusion bands led by Hancock, Miles, and George Duke. The tunes were jams based on composed tunes, which the musicians then overlaid afterward with all sorts of instruments; Zawinul himself is credited with everything from his Rhodes and acoustic piano to TONTO and ARP synthesizers to eclectic instruments like the oud, melodica, steel drums, and the "mzuthra," a one-of-a-kind instrument made by a fan that combined a zither with an African mbira, or thumb piano.[19] *Tale Spinnin'* feels like a warm breeze as if you're drinking rum punch at the beach while an Afro-Latin band plays with astonishing chops and a somewhat eccentric taste in melody.

When *Black Market* arrived on the record-buying market in 1976, Zawinul and Shorter were still firmly in control of the band; they'd each written all but two of the tracks, with one more by Johnson, who had already given notice that he was leaving the band. Even more, the album had no set drummer, with Mahavishnu Orchestra's Narada Michael Walden on a pair of tracks, and Frank Zappa's Chester Thompson on the others. Like *Tale Spinnin'*, this new LP had a humid, lush sound layered over Johnson's trademark bass throb and the Latin percussion of Peruvian Alex Acuña. It was yet another Weather Report album that brilliantly finessed grooves, improvisation, and tight composition into a completely accessible whole.

Black Market was a watershed moment for Weather Report because of the bassist who replaced Johnson, appearing on just two of the tracks: Jaco Pastorius. With him in the lineup, a third distinctive genius was in the Weather Report fold, and with his prowess and showmanship he elevated the group to the level of rock stars in the years ahead. Pastorius grew up around Fort Lauderdale, Florida, the oldest of a single mom's three boys. Seemingly a prodigy at everything he touched, he picked up the bass as a teen. Like so many master musicians, he found an instrument that was a perfect match. He put in the hours learning how to play it while listening to funk and pop records, and by the start of the 1970s, he began playing gigs in various bands to make a name for himself and to support his young wife and daughter. As he played with more and more musicians, his connections grew, and soon Bobby Colomby of jazz-rock legends Blood, Sweat, and Tears got him signed to Epic Records.[20] By late 1975, he was recording his self-titled solo album, which was released the following summer.

If all this sounds like a whirlwind rise, that's because Pastorius was a whirlwind musician. Just one listen to *Jaco Pastorius* (1976) confirms just how revolutionary his sound was on the bass. The first track, a cover of Charlie Parker's "Donna Lee," is just him playing solo, rumbling and popping on just four strings, but somehow sounding like three players on lead, rhythm, and harmonic sound effects. Just as Parker revolutionized the saxophone, Pastorius is making sure you know he's revolutionizing his instrument. His fretless bass allowed him to slide between notes and achieve a liquid intonation that can sound like a bubbling stream or the hubbub of human conversation. Pastorius could play deep funk, jazzy basslines, and sparkling harmonics created by hovering his fingers by just a hair's breadth on the strings. And yet, as Weather Report biographer Curt Bianchi describes it, his instrument was hardly high-tech: "[H]e used a beat-up, old sunburst Fender Jazz bass on which the frets had been removed. He filled the empty slots with wood filler (which left lines on the neck, helping with intonation) and then applied several coats of epoxy to the fretboard to protect it from wear caused by the roundwound strings that he favored." The trick, Pastorius would say, was in how you touched those strings and made them sing.[21]

Pastorius also possessed a brash personality that could easily catch people off-guard. Even Zawinul, the ultimate alpha male, was put off when Pastorius introduced himself a couple of years earlier, after a Weather Report gig in Miami as "John Francis Pastorius III . . . the greatest bass player in the world." Zawinul's response? "Get the fuck away from me." That was 1974, but even if Zawinul thought this in-your-face bassist was a bit crazy, he was completely sold the next year when he heard "Donna Lee" on a rough mix of Pastorius's solo album.[22] With Johnson already departing Weather Report at the time of *Black Market*, Pastorius joined the band, but not before demanding management to get his bass-showcase tune "Barbary Coast" added to the album. As drummer Alex Acuña recalled to Bianchi, "The management said, 'Are you crazy? This is Weather Report—Joe and Wayne. There are no other composers who can write better music than these guys.'"[23] But Pastorius was clear: no tunes, no bass. And it would prove a very wise move that Weather Report relented on both counts. "Barbary Coast" was three minutes of fretless bass as a lead instrument, its sound bubbling over with infectious energy, melodic invention, and a mind-boggling technique that would influence thousands of musicians in the decades ahead, whether in funk or soul or metal.

The first album that the band recorded entirely with Pastorius, *Heavy Weather*, came out in 1977, and in addition to catapulting Weather Report to a new level of stardom, it also introduced a new sound. Instead of airy abstraction or earthy grooves, *Heavy Weather* was agleam with glossy electronic keyboards and superhuman bass. In addition to its leadoff track, the smash hit "Birdland," the mesmerizing ballad "The

Remark You Made" and Pastorius's playful "Teen Town" also became Weather Report staples. Overall, it's a bright, accessible record, but one that risks coming off as too smooth.

Indeed, that was the fate of its follow-up, *Mr. Gone* (1978), an overwhelmingly electronic album of angular melodies and wiggly grooves that sounds weird and intriguing now, but was seen as slick and sterile when it came out. *DownBeat* gave it only one star, and while the album deserved better, the review was prescient in describing the negativity surrounding jazz fusion, by comparing it to an earlier bandleader known for sanitizing big-band jazz: "Weather Report has done to jazz in the seventies what Paul Whiteman did to it in the twenties. Like Whiteman, Weather Report has over-orchestrated its sound. Where Whiteman's band made hot jazz saccharine, Weather Report has made experimentation sound processed."[24] In the irreverent rock magazine *Creem*, Richard C. Walls best expressed how the synthesizer-driven *Mr. Gone* felt like a final break from jazz: "It's avant-garde disco ... The sound [Zawinul] gets is upbeat and extroverted, but the blendings are subtle, and on first hearing, sometimes chilling."[25]

Recorded live in front of a small studio audience, *Night Passage* (1980) was corrective, more organic and fresh than *Mr. Gone*. Weather Report finally had stability in the drum chair for a while with Peter Erskine. An easy-going band member who worked hard to keep up with the machismo and intensity of the band, he could play the drums with incredible force or gentle finesse. This became the most famous iteration of Weather Report, as they filled auditoriums and concert halls around North America, Europe, Japan, and Australia. Zawinul thrilled audiences with the kaleidoscopic synthesizer sound, while Pastorius played the role of the rock star, showcasing his joy on stage by bouncing and gliding to his roiling grooves; the crew would even sprinkle baby powder on his part of his stage to help him slide on his feet.[26] Only Shorter remained diffident in posture, if not in what he played. The best way to truly hear this band on record was the 1979 live double album *8:30*, and *Live and Unreleased* (2002), which compiled recordings from 1975 to 1983. Here, nothing sounds overprocessed at all. The energy level is high, and Shorter sounds like a force of nature, playing with the passion that had seemed to be ebbing from his work in the studio.

Unfortunately, Shorter was starting to withdraw from the band, especially when writing and recording the albums. It must have been tiring to deal with the alpha-male battles that took place between Pastorius and Zawinul, aka the self-proclaimed best bass player on the planet and the self-proclaimed baddest motherfucker on the planet. But Shorter was dealing with many life changes and challenges: coping with a drinking problem, becoming a devoted Nichiren Buddhist, and struggling to raise his daughter, Iska, who was unable to speak or walk due to years of childhood seizures. "It was very painful trying to write, for the first time," he told his biographer Mercer. "I've heard about painters who would stop in the middle of the canvas and say, 'That's all ... I have nothing more to paint.' That's how I felt."[27] Meanwhile, Pastorius's increasingly erratic and tempestuous behavior showed up both off and on stage, where he upstaged and irritated his bandmates by playing too many notes. After an October 1978 gig in Newcastle, a reporter for the British magazine *Sounds* witnessed the road crew carrying a huge flight case that bore the label "Jaco's Ego."[28] He was abusing drugs and alcohol, and he was also dealing with severe bipolar disorder, which wouldn't be diagnosed until he was hospitalized years later. Ever ferociously indefatigable, even Zawinul knew the end was near. He and Pastorius eventually locked horns too many times, their competition and one-upmanship turning from healthy to unpleasant. When Pastorius decided he wanted to form his own band, playing only his compositions, Zawinul and Shorter let him go.[29] Pastorius joined them for one last release: a second album called *Weather Report* (1982) that deliberately bookended their career with another self-titled LP.[30] The record is comparatively pedestrian, an anticlimax for one of the biggest and most exciting bands in jazz.

But as it turned out, Zawinul and Shorter couldn't quit the band just yet. In 1982, they were still contracted to do a summer tour,[31] so they brought in a funky young rhythm section, drummer Omar Hakim and bassist Victor Bailey. Along with percussionists José Rossy and Mino Cinélu, they recorded three inessential but enjoyable albums—*Procession* (1983), *Domino Theory* (1984), and *Sportin' Life* (1985)—that increasingly approached electronic pop-funk. The contract-filling final album, *This Is This!* (1986), is distinguished by being Weather Report's only album with zero compositions by Shorter—and by being the band's worst record by a mile. The back cover features a portrait of Zawinul and Shorter shaking hands on a job well done—with an emphasis on the word "done."

Tragically, Pastorius's career and his short life would soon be over too. After years of drunken and self-destructive behavior, he lost his solo career and even his legendary bass guitar. By

1987, he was back in Fort Lauderdale, penniless and homeless and ravaged by mental illness. On September 12 of that year, he tried to force his way into a nightclub that had banned him for his behavior, whereupon the manager beat him unconscious and fractured his skull. After spending nine days in a coma due to a brain hemorrhage, he died at the age of thirty-five.[32]

Ever the survivor, Zawinul continued to make music for the next twenty years after the last Weather Report album, recording both solo albums and with a new group, the Zawinul Syndicate, that continued to draw audiences if not quite at the same level as Weather Report. By August 2007, however, Zawinul was losing the fight with a rare form of skin cancer. When Shorter got word of Zawinul's dire prognosis, he joined his old partner onstage at a castle in Hungary for one last duet of "In a Silent Way,"[33] and then a month later, the indomitable, seemingly indestructible Austrian was gone.

As for Shorter, he recorded rarely in the 1980s and 1990s, releasing just four solo albums, all unjustly maligned by critics at the time for their heavy use of electronics. It was only at the turn of the millennium, when he turned once again to acoustic jazz, that he regained national treasure status. His Wayne Shorter Quartet would bring him the greatest acclaim and renown of any Weather Report alumnus, and by the time he died at the age of eighty-nine in 2023, he had been nominated for twenty-six Grammys, winning twelve—a grand haul compared to Weather Report's mere six nominations and only one win, for the *8:30* album. One of his final Grammys was for his 2018 triple album, *Emanon*, which was released with a deluxe eighty-four-page sci-fi comic book that Shorter had written about a philosopher fighting against the forces of mental and physical oppression on various worlds. It's both wonderful and inscrutable, just like Shorter himself.

In the end, Weather Report has an outsize role in the history of jazz fusion, one that Zawinul himself could see as early as 1973, when he told a writer from *Rolling Stone*:

> No, I don't think we've left Miles behind. We are just somewhere else, man. Another entity that grew out of him. He's the father and we are the sons, and even when you are small and you stand on the shoulders of the father, you are going to see further than he. That's what we are doing, and one day I hope to have many sons of my own.[34]

Once again, it's a typically cocky statement, but considering the hits Weather Report composed, the sounds they created, and the musicians they influenced over their history and beyond, it's fair to say that they put their legacy where his mouth was.

Ten Essential 1970s Jazz Fusion Albums by the Everchanging Supergroup

- *Super Nova*, by Wayne Shorter (1969)
- *Zawinul*, by Joe Zawinul (1971)
- *Weather Report*, by Weather Report (1971)
- *I Sing the Body Electric*, by Weather Report (1972)
- *Sweetnighter*, by Weather Report (1973)

- *Mysterious Traveller*, by Weather Report (1974)
- *Black Market*, by Weather Report (1976)
- *Jaco Pastorius*, by Jaco Pastorius (1976)
- *Heavy Weather*, by Weather Report (1977)
- *Live and Unreleased*, by Weather Report (2002)

3 The Funky Scientist
Herbie Hancock

Sunlight may not be one of Herbie Hancock's all-time classics, but it is one of his most curious albums. Thirty-nine minutes of synth-jazz fused with funk and disco, it sounds exactly like it came out in 1978, which is not necessarily a bad thing. The album cover feels timebound too: a chic portrait of the artist wearing a medallion, wide-collared black shirt, and an immaculate grey pin-striped suit—tailored by none other than the famed Edward Sexton of Nutters on London's Savile Row.

Even better is the back cover, which not only features the album's lyrics—a first for him—but also shows the musician wearing headphones and engulfed in eleven huge synthesizers. The technology on display here is so vast and astounding that Hancock even lists them all and provides an informational diagram on the inner sleeve: "Oberheim Polyphonic Synthesizer, Obie I, Yamaha CP-30, Hohner D6 Clavinet, ARP 2600, Mini-Moog, ARP String Ensemble, Yamaha Polyphonic Synthesizer and Sequential Circuits Prophet Synthesizer, ARP Odyssey, Poly-Moog, Micro-Moog. Not Shown: Acoustic Piano, E Mu Polyphonic Synthesizer, Rhodes Electric Piano."[1] As Hancock jokes in his memoir, *Possibilities*, "That's a lot for a guy with only two hands!"[2]

Most shockingly, *Sunlight* marks the first time that Hancock sings on record, albeit filtered through electronics. His voice has been encoded and synthesized by a Sennheiser Vocoder VSM 201, a technique that sprays fizzy streams of techno eccentricity across the music's shiny surface. The end result sounds like the robots from Kraftwerk singing and scatting with Kool & the Gang, especially on its lead track, "I Thought It Was You." That song was a hit single in the UK, reaching No. 15 on the charts in August 1978[3] with its futuristic summer vibe, which still sounds effortless despite all the technology that went into it.

Some fans loved seeing him live during the *Sunlight* tour as he took the front of the stage, singing lead and playing a portable keyboard, while jazz snobs registered their hatred of his new phase by booing and leaving. "Those audiences seemed to believe that the artist should be whatever *they* wanted him to do," Hancock recalled, "even if it meant staying stuck in the past. But there was so much new and exciting electronic technology—and so much more on the way—that there was only one way to go, as far as I was concerned: into the future."[4] And there you have it: A mini-manifesto that has guided one of jazz's biggest stars, greatest-ever keyboardists, and most forward thinkers through a career that has thrilled open-minded audiences worldwide, even as it has befuddled and vexed narrower ones.

*****

Herbert Jeffrey Hancock was born in Chicago on April 12, 1940, and as he describes it in his memoir, "we didn't live in the projects but they were close by."[5] His father, Wayman, was a generous soul who sacrificed his own education to help pay for his younger brothers to go to college and had to sell his grocery store because he extended too many people credit.[6] His mother, Winnie, worked as a secretary and then as a guidance counselor for the Illinois State Department of Employment. She strongly believed that her children should be raised with a love of culture, especially classical music. And that meant buying young Herbie a piano. Thankfully, when he was seven years old, they found one for sale in a church basement. In modern music history, it may be the best five dollars ever spent.[7]

Hancock was also a science whiz who loved taking apart mechanisms like clocks and watches and reassembling them to figure out how they worked, and he applied this same approach to mastering his instrument. In fact, he was such a prodigy on the eighty-eight keys that by age eleven, he performed a Mozart concerto with the Chicago Symphony Orchestra. Of course, playing classical music on a page is one thing. Once Hancock heard jazz on local radio, he was eager to learn to improvise, something that did not come naturally at first, so he did the next best thing: turn to science. "I decided to approach improvising the same way I approached taking a clock apart; analytically. I'd find a phrase I liked, and then try to pick out the notes by listening to it over and over—even if just to find a single-note improvisation on the right hand."[8] But even this left-brained approach was insufficient for Hancock, who realized that jazz is "both cerebral and intuitive," a form of music created spontaneously out of such unique transient moments that completely mastering it is inherently impossible. As a result, jazz became something endless to explore, and it pulled him in "like a magnet."[9]

Meanwhile, he advanced his overall education by entering Grinnell College, a renowned liberal arts school in Iowa. In this rural place of rigorous learning, the science-focused Hancock pragmatically chose to major in electrical engineering, pursuing studies that could guarantee him a steadier career than, say, being a jazz musician. But the pull of music wouldn't let him be. As a sophomore, he was organizing Grinnell's first jazz concert, and by his junior year, he'd switched his major to music. Once he started playing gigs in Des Moines, he earned more money than he expected, far more than his day job working in the campus cafeteria. Music began to appear a viable option, and so in 1960, he left college, only one credit short of getting his degree.[10] He would eventually get degrees in both music and electrical engineering from Grinnell, achievements that inspired Joe Zawinul to dedicate one of his best tunes, "Doctor Honoris Causa," to his fellow keyboardist.[11]

Hancock quickly affirmed his leap of faith into jazz. He accelerated through the jazz world over the next decade, as his prodigious talents paid dividends in a whirlwind of gigs. Within weeks of coming home, he was filling in with trumpeter Donald Byrd, who quickly hired him as part of his touring band, brought him to New York, and became a crucial guide for the young pianist in a new city. "I was twenty years old at the time, and Donald kind of took me under his wing," Hancock told reporter Mike Ragogna decades later.

> He and I shared an apartment, and I was kind of like his younger brother. He really watched out for me, nurtured me, and helped me develop. I worked on and off with him for a couple of years, and in the meantime, I got my own record

contract, which Donald was responsible for me getting, and I did a lot of side dates with a lot of people. I got known in New York, where I had moved to when I joined Donald and his band.[12]

That recording contract was with the premier jazz label Blue Note, and by 1962—only two years after he left college—Hancock released his remarkably assured debut album, *Takin' Off*. It featured an all-star band that included Freddie Hubbard on trumpet and Dexter Gordon on sax, but more importantly, it featured "Watermelon Man." Inspired by Hancock's childhood memories, the funky rhythm came from the clacking wheels of a street vendor's watermelon cart in Chicago, while the quirky melody came from the sassy catcalls of the neighborhood women who greeted the watermelon man. Ever aware of his Black identity, Hancock examined whether this image was too much of a caricature of his neighborhood life but decided in the end to reclaim it as a source of pride.[13] "Watermelon Man" was such an irresistible tune that it was released as a single and lifted *Takin' Off* to No. 84 on the Billboard 100 charts.[14] But even more importantly, the following year Cuban percussionist Mongo Santamaria rose to the top ten of the pop charts with a concise version that stripped the improvisation and added Latin percussion and vocals. As the composer earning royalties, Herbie Hancock soon had more financial security than his colleagues.

At the same time that Hancock found fame, Miles Davis found him. Miles met him through Donald Byrd and soon invited him over to his house to jam with bassist Ron Carter and drummer Tony Williams. Miles loved how they sounded together, so he invited Hancock to join them in the recording studio. "So does that mean I'm in the group?" the steady, analytical Hancock asked the man who would become his mercurial mentor. "You're making a record with me, ain't you?" Miles retorted.[15] Once Wayne Shorter came on board, Miles's great Second Quintet was complete, recording their canonical mid-1960s albums that took the familiar melodies and modes of jazz and deconstructed them to create a moody, abstract style.

This spirit of increasing adventurism infused the remarkable run of solo albums Hancock simultaneously recorded for Blue Note in the 1960s. With each of these LPs, Hancock shows great compositional range. On 1964's *Empyrean Isles*, for example, he exuded hard-bop soul on "Cantaloupe Island," but also branched out into fourteen minutes of difficult atonality on "The Egg." He created a whole concept album about the sea on 1965's *Maiden Voyage*, then explored dreamy sonic textures on *Speak Like a Child* (1968) with flugelhorn, bass trombone, and flute. *The Prisoner* (1969) served as a pivot point for Hancock in that it was his clearest expression of his Black identity to date, with the Reverend Martin Luther King Jr.-inspired opener, "I Have a Dream," and the title track addressing how Black people feel in a predominately White society. *The Prisoner* is also Hancock's first record where he plays electric piano, where you can hear the sound of jazz fusion coming around a bend in the road, though not yet on the same block. It was also his first solo album after leaving Miles's quintet. The story goes that Miles was irked when the recently wed Hancock decided to extend his honeymoon in Brazil, so he brought in keyboardist Chick Corea as a replacement. But by this point, Hancock was already so self-assured as a bandleader, arranger, and composer that he was ready to move on anyway.

Indeed, Hancock was a big enough name to land a deal with a major label, and his first Warner Bros. release, *Fat Albert Rotunda* (1969), seemed a curious one on paper. Comedian Bill Cosby was creating an animated TV special called *Hey, Hey, Hey, It's Fat Albert*—based on the kids he grew up with on the streets of North Philadelphia. He filled it with characters such as the goofy Mushmouth and Dumb Donald, all led by a good-natured and rather heavy-set boy named Fat Albert Robertson, and he wanted Hancock to create original music for it. "I mean, I didn't even hesitate," recalled Hancock. "A prime-time cartoon starring Black characters? Created by a Black comedian? That was a really big deal for 1969, so I jumped at Bill's offer."[16]

Hancock recorded *Fat Albert Rotunda* with famed Blue Note engineer Rudy Van Gelder, but otherwise the sound was completely unlike anything he'd done before. His sextet included Joe Henderson on sax and flute, Johnny Coles on trumpet and flugelhorn, Garnett Brown on trombone, Tootie Heath on drums, and Buster Williams, who played both acoustic and electric bass. With the story set in Philly, Hancock felt the music should lean hard into R&B. "We stayed pretty close to the sensibility of James Brown," Garnett Brown told jazz historian Bob Gluck. "This was really bread and butter for those New York musicians who were known for their specialties in rhythm and blues and pop."[17] With song titles like "Wiggle-Waggle" and "Fat Mama," the album is joyous and buoyant, and to generations raised on the *Fat Albert* cartoon series that came later, these tracks burst with the technicolor and life of the characters. Audiences at the Fillmore East rock club certainly felt it in

December 1970, as *DownBeat* reported Hancock earning "stomping, standing ovations" from the counterculture crowd. "His avowed ambition is to reach just about everybody and to break down the barriers created by musical labels," the magazine reported. "*Fat Albert Rotunda* shows he's the man who can do it."[18]

And yet, that's what Hancock proceeded *not* to do. Instead, he went on to make his wildest music, rearranging the molecules of jazz fusion with a combination of jazz, electronics, and Afrocentrism—all played by his magisterial new sextet, known in history as the Mwandishi band. The name itself comes from the word for "composer" in Swahili, and Hancock soon assumed it as a title, just as all the other band mates assumed Swahili honorifics: bassist Buster Williams became "Mchezaji," or "the Player"; bass clarinetist Bennie Maupin became "Mwile," or "Body of Good Health," after convincing his bandmates to become vegetarians; "Pepo Mtoto" (Spirit Child) Julian Priester was a trombonist who had played with cosmic free jazz bandleader Sun Ra; trumpeter Eddie Henderson was "Mganga," or "doctor," because of his medical degree; and powerhouse drummer Billy Hart aptly was named "Jabali," or "energy." These names were a statement of Black pride and also a symbol of how the band members fused together on hourlong space-flight group improvisations. "[We] became a unit," Priester told Gluck. "It was like we became a family, you know? We had something in common, as families do."[19]

The great tragedy of the Mwandishi band is that they are woefully under-documented on record, having recorded only three studio albums and released nothing officially from their many long-revered mind-blowing concerts. Thankfully, those three studio albums are so rich in sound and ideas that it's easy to get lost in each one, requiring you to play it again, and then some more. No matter how dense the sound, the heart of it all was Hancock, playing his Fender Rhodes electric piano filtered through gadgets like the Echoplex, a tape delay unit that enabled him to bend pitches and create twinkling notes that sounded like they were scattered out among the stars.

The first of the Mwandishi albums was called just that: *Mwandishi*. Released in 1971, this album included a bass-heavy homage to political activist Angela Davis, played in 15/4 time, and a space-age floater called "You'll Know When You Get There," that began life as a commercial jingle Hancock wrote for Eastern Airlines, strangely enough.[20] It culminated in the twenty-two-minute "Wandering Spirit Song," which starts like an eerie voyage through mystic hills and dales and then explodes into a frenzy of atonal piano clusters splattered with wailing horns, all echoing and reverberating like nighttime phantasms hollering across a river valley. Deservedly, *Mwandishi* was named one of *Time* magazine's albums of the year, but it was too challenging for the pop audiences that Hancock was winning over just a year or so before.

Commercial failure did not stop the Mwandishi band, however, and two important changes happened to Hancock in 1972. The first was musical: While recording the album *Crossings*, his music took a wonderfully weirder turn thanks to technology and Hancock's producer, David Rubinson. "David suggested the synthesizer since it was a new thing, and kind of hot on the pop scene," Hancock explained to writer Julie Coryell in the mid-1970s. "You know everybody was into acid—it was kind of associated with acid and freakiness and all that."[21] Ever the electrical engineer, Hancock had even visited techies at MIT in Boston, who showed him how he could change the shape of sound waves.[22] So Hancock followed Rubinson's suggestion and took his tapes to a tech whiz in San Francisco named Patrick Gleeson and let him overdub all sorts of synthesizer sounds as an experiment. Hancock loved the results so much, he let Gleeson work on *Crossings* and its follow-up, *Sextant* (1973), and brought him on the road as a live jazz synth soundscaper.

With *Crossings* as his first take on synthesizers in fusion, Hancock eschewed an idea of the pop scene and veered hard into freakiness. The first half of the album is taken up by the twenty-five-minute "Sleeping Giant," a title that references Africa arising from centuries of colonialism. This mind-melting colossus begins with a whirlwind of skittering, chattering percussion before the familiar Echoplexed piano enters. From then on, the listener is swept away in a multipart suite that tosses you from extended piano solos to bustling grooves to spacey horn-led interludes to a jumped-up fuzz-bass jam to a duet of just bass and soprano sax. Side two boasts two extended abstract tracks that meld acoustic piano, fluttering flute, bass clarinet, alien synthesizers, and disembodied voices, conjuring up brief flares of light that quickly dissipate into the menacing dark noise of synthesized space. *Crossings* still sounds astonishing today, but was too much so back then for Warner Bros., who released Hancock from his contract. He then switched to Columbia Records, who distributed his records through the next decade.

The second major change for Hancock in 1972 was spiritual. For months, he had been enraptured by Buster Williams's superhuman bass playing in concert, which was so inspired it seemed almost divine. Finally, after one show in Seattle, Hancock recalled that Williams revealed the creative strength and enlightenment he received from Buddhism: "During those two hours when the rest of us were sleeping off the previous night's partying, Buster had been awake in his room, chanting the words *Nam Myoho Renge Kyo* over and over. He hadn't slept at all, but when it came time for the gig, he had more energy than all the rest of us put together."[23] Intrigued, Hancock embarked on a journey in Nichiren Buddhism, a rigorous spiritual practice of this ancient faith whose tenets—put absurdly simply here—include chanting as a means of enlightenment, intense study of the spiritual texts of the ancient Buddhist priest Nichiren, and sharing the faith in order to further prosperity and peace in humanity. Much like his friend Wayne Shorter, Hancock had Nichiren Buddhism as a vital spiritual base in both his creative and personal life.

For his next album, *Sextant*, Hancock listed the hardware he used, including keyboards like the Hohner D-6 Clavinet and Mellotron and electronics like ARP synthesizers and a Random Resonator. It all signaled that this would be an even more extreme album, layered with synthesized plink-plonks that sound like electronic rain, cacophonous blasts of electric piano and horns, atonal robot riffs, mechanical birdcalls, and off-kilter rhythms that often feel like the horns are playing in a totally different time signature from the rhythm section. On the final twenty-minute track, "Hornets," an insistent bass riff rumbles along as Hancock jams on a clavinet, and the band uses a host of instruments to create the vibe of an urban rainforest on the edge of a galaxy. If there's anything that sounds familiar at all here, it's a similarity to the most extreme albums from Miles's electric period—which makes sense, as Hancock, Maupin, and Hart of the Mwandishi band were among the uncredited musicians who contributed to Miles's throbbing funktronic masterpiece *On the Corner*.[24]

These Mwandishi masterworks may combine the ghostly funk of Sly and the Family Stone's *There's a Riot Goin' On* with the complex prog-rock pomp of Pink Floyd and Yes, but these albums didn't sell anywhere near that level, and Hancock came to a painful realization that he was both losing money and had hit a creative end with the Mwandishi band. "When I started the sextet," Hancock recalled in his memoir, "I was eager to become untethered musically, and when we first did, it was thrilling. But Mwandishi's music became so spacey, and so far out, that after a while it got exhausting. Now I wanted to make music that was more rhythmic, music that would connect me back to the earth."[25]

Exit the freakiness of the Mwandishi band and enter Hancock's other great group of the 1970s, the Headhunters band. With the exception of Bennie Maupin on reeds, this group was entirely new: session veteran Harvey Mason Sr. on drums; Bill Summers, a U.C. Berkeley student of Afro-Cuban and West African ethnomusicology,[26] on percussion; and the great bassist Paul Jackson anchoring the bottom end. With Gleeson gone, Hancock played all the synths as well as the pianos and keyboards. "The original goal was [that] I wanted to make a funk album that had nothing to do with jazz," Hancock told Cornell music professor Steven F. Pond. "But, you see, in the development, it kind of took on its own character, which was unique."[27] What he didn't know then was that when *Head*

Hunters came out in the fall of 1973, it would rock the *Billboard* charts, reaching No. 1 in jazz, No. 2 in R&B, and No. 13 in the overall pop charts. It would stay on the charts for almost an entire calendar year and be certified platinum[28]—not bad for a new artistic shift.

A sticky hybrid of funk and jazz, *Head Hunters* was unclassifiable. Its famous opening track, "Chameleon," is sixteen minutes of deep and dirty funk, based around an easy-loping synthesizer bassline that locks in with a Mason backbeat that keeps the whole tune nestled deeply in his pocket. The band keeps adding on layers: Jackson's high-pitched bass picking, massed horns, and then Hancock's completely wigged-out extended solo on an ARP Odyssey synthesizer. Almost eight minutes in, the tune shifts to incorporate a pulsing Jackson bassline, and Hancock delivers a smooth extended solo on the Fender Rhodes. By the end, this brilliant tune has returned to the synth bass and a Maupin solo on sax, and you find that you've been dancing all along with your headphones on. Surprisingly, it's followed by a relaxed remake of Hancock's first hit, "Watermelon Man," except this version begins with Summers blowing on a beer bottle, making it sound like a resonant whistle and basing the pattern on traditional calls of Ba-Benzélé pygmies.[29] There's nothing relaxed about "Sly," a fast and furious funk workout that leaves the listener breathless, while the finale, "Vein Melter," brings the heat down to a glorious slow-jam simmer.

Head Hunters was such a mammoth success that one can easily excuse Hancock for making roughly the same record the following year with *Thrust* (1974), packed with playful melodies and relentless sassy funk. The album was a hit on all the same charts, proving that *Head Hunters* wasn't just a one-off. Though *Man-Child* (1975) didn't climb as high as *Head Hunters* or *Thrust*, it broadened Hancock's sound with an expanded horn section starring old friend Wayne Shorter on sax; electric guitarists like Motown veteran Wah Wah Watson and Blackbyrd McKnight, who would later play in Parliament-Funkadelic; and even Stevie Wonder playing some hurricane-force harmonica. A more laidback album, *Secrets* (1976) continued Hancock's gentle slide down to the Top 50 of the pop charts, but it boasts a career highlight in the seven-minute "People Music," an astonishing suite that sounds like a journey from an LA sunset grill to the furthest quasars and spirit temples at the end of the universe. This era also features a live document called *Flood*, originally released in Japan in 1975. Recorded in Tokyo, it shows how the band took their intensity up to an even higher plane in concert, particularly Hancock, who flies his hands all over his electronic equipment. One can hear how much this electrical engineering major is thrilled to play with seemingly limitless pitches, timbres, and tones.

As Hancock closed out the 1970s, his jazz fusion records achieved a comfortable and consistent commercial position within the top 100 of the pop charts and the top 40 of R&B, and they continued to top the jazz charts, even as they veered even further from the recognizable jazz idiom. *Sunlight* came in 1978 with its dance-driven sound and Vocoder singing, then Hancock leaped fully into commercial pop with *Feets Don't Fail Me Now* (1979), which applied an odd stew of disco, lounge music, electrofunk, and group vocals to surprisingly flat tunes. March 1980 welcomed the middling *Monster*, which added rock and Latin music to the disco mix, and in October Hancock brought out the excellent *Mr. Hands*, an eclectic release that sounded smooth like *Secrets* on one track and bouncy like *Thrust* on the next.

Amid all these pop experiments and accessible tunes, one could ask how much of this could be called jazz. *Phonograph Record* critic Colman Andrews had the best answer back in 1974:

> Roughly, Herbie Hancock is still a jazz musician, I think. True, he may freely adapt elements of electronic music and progressive rock into his playing and writing, and he may frequently patch them into (and *set* them into) an idiom which sounds suspiciously like something we could call rhythm-and-blues. But he and his fellow musicians draw most strongly on the features of jazz music—linear improvisation, jazz-steeped instrumental attacks and tonal qualities, and good, old-fashioned *swing*.[30]

The irony is that Hancock was so prolific in the 1970s that, even amid all his jazz fusion albums and his soundtracks for movies like the Charles Bronson thriller *Death Wish* (1974), he still returned to good, old-fashioned jazz. At a retrospective concert for the Newport Jazz Festival that he staged at New York City Center on June 29, 1976, Hancock performed separate sets with each of the three bands that had shaped him as a musician and made him a star: Miles's Second Quintet, but with Freddie Hubbard on trumpet (Miles declined to appear); the Mwandishi band; and the final version of the Headhunters that had appeared on *Secrets*. The show and the resulting live double album were called *V.S.O.P.*, which stood for both the high grade of cognac that has improved with age and an acronym for "Very Special Onetime Performance." The Quintet reunion became a long-term affair[31]—and so, even at the height of his forays into electrofunk and disco in the late 1970s, he was touring and recording acoustic jazz with Freddie Hubbard, Wayne Shorter, Ron Carter, and Tony Williams.

Hancock's career ever since is distinguished by such eclectic productivity. In the 1980s, he shocked the jazz world and rocked the pop charts once again by incorporating hip-hop into his music. "Rockit," the lead single off *Future Shock* (1983), startled the airwaves with turntable scratches by Grand Mixer DST, and with a music video, directed by Kevin Godley and Lol Creme, that featured a house filled with animatronic robots all dancing to the beat-heavy banger. In the same era, though, he was the musical director on record and on screen for Bernard Tavernier's 1986 Oscar-nominated movie *Round Midnight*, about a troubled aging jazzman, played by the same bebop legend Dexter Gordon who had played on Hancock's solo debut almost 25 years earlier. The following decade, he would be happy to record *Gershwin's World* (1998), a tribute to the great American composer, and then follow it up three years later with a drum-and-bass record called *Future2Future*. Pop and acoustic jazz converged for Hancock in 2007 with *River: The Joni Letters*, a tribute album to songwriting legend Joni Mitchell. A complete artistic triumph, it took home two honors at the Fiftieth Grammy Awards: Best Contemporary Jazz Album and the prestigious Album of the Year.

All along, there have been those grumblings and questions about Hancock's crazy quilt of a career: How could someone so masterful at composing jazz classics and playing acoustic piano have gone so far astray? Famed *Village Voice* jazz critic

Gary Giddins once wrote about how Hancock's work with Miles's Second Quintet continued to inspire younger musicians, only to offer this uncharitable aside about the attitudes of jazz purists: "If Hancock had gone to the great beyond in 1968, he would now be solemnly regarded as a jazz god."[32] But Hancock the scientist was never going to stop experimenting, and Hancock the Buddhist was never going to stop searching. As he told Julie Coryell back in the 1970s:

> [Buddhism] accelerates the process of learning about life in general—the world—the universe that we live in . . . You can change your character and, at the same time, change your fortune. And what happened is that through chanting, I began to find out more about myself, and the reason I'm playing this music is not because chanting told me to play it; it's only because I discovered that this is the music I like to play.[33]

In short, why be just a jazz god when you can be so much more?

Ten Essential 1970s Jazz Fusion Albums by the Funky Scientist

Fat Albert Rotunda (1969)
Mwandishi (1971)
Crossings (1972)
Sextant (1973)
Head Hunters (1973)

Thrust (1974)
Flood (1975)
Man-Child (1975)
Secrets (1976)
Mr. Hands (1980)

4 Three Loud Visionaries
Tony Williams, John McLaughlin, and Chick Corea

When a young boy named Anthony Tillmon Williams was growing up in Boston in the 1950s, he taught himself how to play drums while his father brought him to club gigs on the weekends. By 1954, at just nine years old, young Tony joined in with the band, playing dance tunes or radio hits of the time. Before long, he was the main attraction. As he recalled later in the 1970s,

> I remember after I'd get through playing a couple numbers all the people in the place would really like it, a little kid playing the drums. So they would give me money, and at the end of some of the nights I'd have more money than the guys in the band. I'd get thirty-five dollars in one night, and the guys in the band were working for fifteen or twenty dollars.[1]

Still only a tweener, Williams took lessons from Berklee professor Alan Dawson and soon had a reputation as one of the best drummers in the city. Then on December 17, 1962—a mere five days after his seventeenth birthday—Williams met up with hard-bop sax star Jackie McLean at Connolly's Stardust Room in Roxbury, the heart of Boston's Black community. According to Boston jazz historian Richard Vacca, McLean was a featured soloist in need of a local rhythm section, and Williams's power and creativity were already so apparent that McLean invited him to come play in New York. After permission from his mom, Williams was off to the Big Apple and immediately made an impression on the biggest names in the business.[2] "I had heard this great little seventeen-year-old drummer who was working with Jackie McLean named Tony Williams, who just blew my fucking mind," Miles Davis recalled with typical candor in his autobiography. "[T]rumpet players love to play with great drummers and I could definitely hear right away that this was going to be one of the baddest motherfuckers who had ever played a set of drums."[3] Within months, Williams joined what would become Miles's revered Second Quintet and performed on the album *Seven Steps to Heaven*. When Williams returned to Boston in January 1964, as Vacca notes wryly, he was playing Symphony Hall.[4]

So what made this teenager so good that he so swiftly rocketed to the pinnacle of America's greatest art form? First off, he could just whack the shit out of the drums. But he was also a supremely intelligent musician with advanced ideas on meter and pulse and using every technique to create new textured sounds on the drums. For example, few drummers could create a whole polyrhythmic soundworld out of shimmering cymbals and open hi-hats quite like Williams. As future Miles bassist Dave Holland would tell journalist Alyn Shipton decades later, "I would say that Tony Williams was the focal point for the band's rhythmic development. If you discuss this with Herbie [Hancock], he speaks of Tony as being a very important influence on him, as to how he approached rhythm—it really changed his approach to how to use the piano rhythmically."[5] So it's no surprise that such an advanced musician was also a composer, and that by the summer of 1964, he was already recording his first solo album, *Life Time*.

As it turns out, Lifetime was also the name of the pioneering electric band that Williams would form upon leaving Miles's Second Quintet in 1968. Both he and Miles shared a love of Jimi Hendrix, Sly Stone, and James Brown, but Williams was far more interested in rock. He loved not only the experimentation of the Beatles but also the force of hard rock, exemplified by the power-trio supergroup Cream and the anarchic proto-punks MC5.[6] After all, it's worth remembering that by this point Williams had just entered his twenties, while Miles was his fortysomething boss—albeit the coolest fortysomething boss ever. As a young rock fan, Williams was eager to explore free jazz improvisation at maximum volume, so in forming his new band, he hired a buzzed-about new electric guitarist out of London named John McLaughlin and then added the otherworldly organist Larry Young. As Williams reflected on his departure two decades later, "I left Miles' band because I thought it was important to start making the mistakes I was bound to make and be young enough to bounce back."[7]

The result was Lifetime's double album *Emergency!* (1969), one of the most influential jazz fusion albums ever made and also one of the first to usher in the concept of jazz-rock. Despite being an artistic landmark, however, it's always been quite a hard sell to casual listeners. First off, the sound is terrible, like it was recorded on discs of wet cardboard. Furthermore, this ferocious band is more focused on blasting incendiary riffs than crafting memorable tunes; they make contemporary power trios like Cream, the Jimi Hendrix Experience, and Emerson, Lake & Palmer sound genteel by comparison. Despite these challenges, *Emergency!* is brilliant, just an explosion of pure energy expressed in a sound completely unique, conceived by a musician who loved rock and free jazz and cutting-edge composers like Bartók, Stravinsky, and Stockhausen.[8] Williams plays gargantuan rhythms on his drums that he keeps breaking up with rapid-fire fills and mind-spinning syncopated embellishments, while McLaughlin sparks hot fire from his guitar and takes these songs into some thrillingly raw places. Unfairly overlooked in the annals of jazz history, organist Larry Young is the glue here, expanding the sound with huge, sustained block chords, frenzied free soloing, fast hard-bop soul grooves, and cathedrals of atonal sound. By the time *Emergency!*'s relentlessly monumental and inventive seventy minutes of avant-garde proto-metal jazz-rock are over, the disoriented listener is either exhausted or exhilarated, or both.

On Lifetime's follow-up, *Turn It Over* (1970), the band smashes apart song structure until it's unrecognizable, some of it sounding like the Velvet Underground's "Sister Ray" done fusion-style. McLaughlin and Williams continued to duel each other in volume and in speed, while Young—now known by his Islamic name Khalid Yasin—continued to rage on the organ. New member Jack Bruce, fresh off his superstar stint with Cream, joined in with buzzing bass and virtuoso technique that fills in the empty spaces already not filled in by the others. But when Williams put together *Ego* in 1971, Lifetime was a much more relaxed beast, based more on polyrhythmic percussion and handclaps than scorching electric feedback. McLaughlin was gone, and Young/Yasin remained in a subdued role on organ. Though not as confrontational as the first two Lifetime records, *Ego* is still just as strange and intriguing.

For those three albums alone, Williams's place in the pantheon of jazz-rock giants is secure. But for the rest of the 1970s, Williams kept changing his music to sound like everybody else, and it didn't work. He formed a completely new version of Lifetime in 1975, but albums like *Believe It* (1975) and *Million Dollar Legs* (1976) were at best serviceable and at worst the kind of anonymously proficient music that naysayers think of when they hear the phrase "jazz fusion." He did close out the decade with a solo album called *The Joy of Flying* (1978), which boasted an all-star cast including Herbie Hancock and fellow Headhunter Paul Jackson, Return to Forever bassist Stanley Clarke, saxmen like David Sanborn and Michael Brecker, and guitarist George Benson. It's easy to enjoy, and also easy to forget once it's over. It was a troublesome end to the decade after such a thrilling start. As writer Stuart Nicholson cogently and concisely put it, "His predicament was that his adventurous past was writ so large that it tended to diminish anything new that he attempted."[9]

Still, throughout the 1980s and 1990s, he remained one of the most open-minded musicians in jazz, even when he returned to acoustic albums. He loved new wave music like the Police and Missing Persons and even played live with avant-garde electronic artist Laurie Anderson.[10] But tragically, just as Williams entered the jazz world at a young age, he left the corporeal world early as well. On February 23, 1997, he died of a heart attack two days after undergoing gallbladder surgery. He was merely fifty-one years old. His sudden death robbed the world of a musical titan who spurned jazz purism and never shied away from trying to reach wider audiences with his music. "Jazz was originally the music of the people in the streets and not in concert halls, so when you lose that, you suffer the consequences," Williams told *DownBeat* in 1983. "There's nothing wrong with jazz being an art form, but it has a certain roughness and vitality and unexpectedness that's important." And then he added, "I guess I'm old-fashioned."[11] He must have meant that last part ironically, because, of course, he was anything but.

*****

John McLaughlin had to make a choice. The year was 1969, and he had arrived in the jazz epicenter, New York City. The previous few years, he'd been building a reputation in the UK as a guitarist who could seamlessly blend jazz and rock and fuse them into something hard, intense, and new. So in October 1968, he sat in on a jam at Ronnie Scott's club in London with new Miles Davis bassist Dave Holland and American drummer Jack DeJohnette. A bootleg recording found its way to Tony Williams, who was so thrilled upon hearing it that in January he invited McLaughlin across the pond to join his new group, Lifetime. Upon arrival in the Big Apple, Williams took him up to Harlem to jam at the Club Baron and then brought him to visit Miles Davis. Miles liked the twenty-seven-year-old[12] Brit and invited him to bring his guitar to the recording studio. Yes, on just his third day in the United States, McLaughlin found himself playing on the seminal *In a Silent Way*.[13] By the end of the year, he would record key parts on two more pioneering jazz fusion albums: *Emergency!* and *Bitches Brew*. The problem was that both leaders wanted him in each of their bands permanently. So McLaughlin had to make a choice, one that any musician would envy. He chose the riskier path: the young Williams and the untested Lifetime.

"It was the best of all worlds," McLaughlin told *DownBeat* in 1978.

> But by this time, Lifetime with Larry Young was underway. I thought that Larry was the greatest organ player in the world . . . So here was my favorite organist with my favorite drummer. I was in the perfect set-up. We were making pennies, but I felt it to be a part of my destiny. The most unexpected thing in my life was for me to turn Miles down because Miles was my idol. I'd been listening to Miles since I was 15.[14]

Young John McLaughlin was born in 1942 near Doncaster in Yorkshire, but he spent his teenage years in the North East England conurbation of Newcastle-upon-Tyne. His guides to this new world of music were his two older brothers, who not only got him his first guitar but also introduced him to American bluesmen like Muddy Waters and Sonny Terry. At age fourteen, he heard an album by American jazz guitarist Tal Farlow playing in a Newcastle record store, and he got hooked on jazz. Already hyper-disciplined about practicing, McLaughlin was such a prodigy that when he briefly took lessons, his guitar instructor was more interested in listening to him than teaching him.[15] Still a teenager in 1959, he left home for the big city—in this case, London—where he first got a job selling guitars at Selmer's music shop on Charing Cross Road. He demonstrated the guitars by jamming on them, and soon enough, he gained a reputation for being that young salesman with the astonishing skills.[16]

By the early 1960s, he had played in bands like Georgie Fame and the Blue Flames, the Brian Auger Group, and the Graham Bond Quartet—the latter of which also included future Cream stars Ginger Baker and Jack Bruce and that even then was playing a hybrid of jazz with rock energy. He also became an in-demand session musician, where he earned the distinction of playing guitar on the second-ever recorded Beatles cover, "I Saw Her Standing There," sung by the long-forgotten popstar Duffy Power in 1963.[17] As the decade wore on, McLaughlin moved around, acquiring eclectic achievements, from playing in the orchestra for the *Ready Steady Go!* TV show to giving guitar lessons to future Led Zeppelin rock god Jimmy Page.[18] By the tail end of the decade, McLaughlin was worn out by endless session work, but he had enough of a name to record his debut solo album, *Extrapolation*, in early 1969. With a clean, less frantic tone here, McLaughlin sounds startlingly different from the later work that would make him famous. But the latent energy is still there, as is the dreamy soulfulness and allusions to South Asian drones and scales that would become his trademark.

Once McLaughlin settled in the United States, he found that Lifetime may have been thrilling, but it struggled to reach a broader audience. So he continued to go into the studio with his icon Miles, notably playing guitar on *A Tribute to Jack Johnson* (1971) and *Big Fun* (1974), where he enjoyed a long six-string showcase, playfully named "Go Ahead John." And he also continued to record albums under his own name. The chunky, electric fuzz of *Devotion* (1970) was a true volte-face from the lithe jazz of *Extrapolation*, while *My Goals Beyond* (1971) was split between lovely solo-guitar miniatures and sonorous prog rock laced with Indian tablas and droning tamburas.

The Beatles and their famous 1968 trek to Maharishi Mahesh Yogi's ashram in Rishikesh will always be the most famous celebrity pilgrimage, but the visit mostly reflected how Indian music and culture were then trending in psychedelia. McLaughlin's involvement was hardly an act of being trendy, as he went through one of the most important changes in his life in the last months of the 1960s. He became a disciple of Sri Chinmoy, a spiritual leader who had attracted followers over the past decade through writings and lectures about how to promote peace, how to have a healthy mind and body, how self-realization is God-realization, and how to find joy in the inner life of prayer and meditation.[19]

McLaughlin met Chinmoy while he was guesting on Larry Coryell's *Spaces* in March 1969. As one who also melded blazing rock and fluid jazz, Coryell had a similar musical spirit. Even though he never enjoyed mainstream success, he remained an insider's influence on guitarists, so much so that six-string star Al Di Meola would dub him "the Godfather of Fusion" in the late 1970s.[20] But in the winter of 1969, Coryell was also launching his career, and he was flabbergasted as he watched this new British musician play at Count Basie's club in Harlem. After thirty seconds of McLaughlin's first solo, Coryell turned to his wife Julie and told her that this had to be the best guitar player he'd seen in his life.[21] So Coryell invited him to the studio, and while they were recording, the album's producer, Danny Weiss, invited the two guitarists to see Chinmoy speak in Connecticut.[22] McLaughlin had already been studying yoga and Asian religions, and as he put it, he was a disciple ready for his master to appear. Sri Chinmoy quickly became that master, guiding McLaughlin through much of the 1970s and bestowing his famous axe-slinging acolyte with the honorific name Mahavishnu.

The other major change for McLaughlin had to do with his career. By April 1971, his time in Lifetime was over, so he set about gathering a group of talented, intense musicians. Two appeared on the electric side of *My Goals Beyond*: drummer Billy Cobham, who he'd seen playing with Horace Silver in London, and then violinist Jerry Goodman from the American prog group the Flock. After McLaughlin recruited bassist Rick Laird, who had played with him in the Brian Auger Group, Weather Report's Miroslav Vitouš recommended a fellow Czech named Jan Hammer, a flamboyant keyboardist who would become most famous in the 1980s for recording the TV theme song for *Miami Vice*. All the band needed was a name, and Sri Chinmoy provided it: Mahavishnu Orchestra.[23] They mesmerized audiences because every member of the band was overflowing with outrageous pomp and energy. McLaughlin took center stage, blazing on the guitar, but Cobham matched him with polyrhythmic hurricanes, Goodman made his violin scream with spiraling solos, and Hammer spun dizzying runs on his Fender Rhodes and Moog synthesizer. Put together, they sounded even more massive than the sum of their parts.

This revered incarnation of the Mahavishnu Orchestra lasted a mere three years and produced only three albums. But what brilliant albums of electric power and spiritual grace! *The Inner Mounting Flame* (1971) and *Birds of Fire* (1973) are the two studio albums that just about every jazz-rock fan has in their collection; the latter reached No. 15 on the *Billboard* pop charts[24] and eventually went gold.[25] The Mahavishnu Orchestra set the standard at the very start of *The Inner Mounting Flame.* "The Meeting of the Spirits" begins with a long, hazy intro that crescendos until it explodes into mayhem, and on "The Noonward Race," Hammer even outpaces McLaughlin by playing a delirious solo on his Fender Rhodes and warping the sound with a ring modulator. *Birds of Fire* blasts off with the insistently ascending riffs of the title track and rarely lets up; even the seemingly bucolic "Open Country Joy" breaks open into hard-rock fever. Aptly enough, the band then went on tour with rock stars who could match their feverish energy, such as Santana, Emerson, Lake & Palmer, and Jeff Beck. And wherever they went, critics were sure to share in the ecstasy. "McLaughlin's spiritual concerns are inseparable from his music, and a Mahavishnu Orchestra concert is as much a ritual and a devotional service as it is a musical presentation," wrote the *Los Angeles Times*'s Richard Cromelin about a 1972 gig at the Santa Monica Civic Auditorium. "All five musicians appear to be transported to a different plane, and one feels that they might in fact be vehicles through which a music from some holy source is being poured. It isn't namby-pamby religio-rock, though, but a gripping tapestry of tension and release, of stunning intensity contrasted with pastoral grace."[26]

For McLaughlin, 1973 brought both turmoil and more brilliant music. First, he recorded an astonishing collaboration with Carlos Santana called *Love Devotion Surrender*, where the two bandleaders collaborated with members of the Mahavishnu Orchestra, the Santana band, and old friend Khalid Yasin on organ. The album's photos featured the two devout guitarists clad in white and posing serenely with Sri Chinmoy, but the album is a fire-breathing beast, where spirituality burns through the volcanic riffs, jazz melodies, Latin rhythms, and cosmic covers of John Coltrane's most famous classics, "A Love Supreme" and "Naima."

Less successful were the June sessions at London's Trident Studios for a third Mahavishnu Orchestra album, which fell apart amid acrimony over McLaughlin's leadership and his unwillingness to record his bandmates' compositions. As bassist Laird told *Rolling Stone* the following year, "That record date was a disaster. We salvaged nothing from it. After five days I remember John leaving the date crying."[27] So instead they scrapped the sessions and recorded most of the material at a concert in New York's Central Park that August. Released later in 1973 as *Between Nothingness and Eternity*, the three long tracks are powerful, but the live sound is raw enough to be distracting, so much so that fans wondered for years if the scrapped studio album was a forever-lost classic à la the Beach Boys' *Smile*. Miraculously, their wishes were granted in 1999 when *The Lost Trident Sessions* was released, which included the studio versions of *Between . . .*'s tunes and a few extras. The studio versions sounded lovely, warm, and crisp, but they lacked the force of the live versions. Sometimes in music, history is not what it's meant to be.

By January 1974, the Mahavishnu Orchestra itself was history. When Cobham gave an interview with *Melody Maker*'s Chris Welch a few weeks later, he called the breakup "a total fiasco because of emotional problems." His hurt emotions were clear as he detailed how the band never traveled together, how communication was bad, how egos formed factions within the band, and how McLaughlin seemed split inside between being a superstar bandleader and a religious disciple. By the end, Cobham said with regret, "No one cared anymore. From there, things became more and more mechanical."[28] For a band whose rocket fuel was pure passion, it appeared they burned themselves to ashes.

And yet the Mahavishnu Orchestra rose, phoenix-like, with McLaughlin fronting a whole new band: Jean-Luc Ponty on electric violin, Gayle Moran on keyboards and vocals, Ralphe Armstrong on bass, and Narada Michael Walden on drums. For Mahavishnu II's first release, *Apocalypse* (1974), McLaughlin went all-out, collaborating with the London Symphony Orchestra and hiring Beatles producer George Martin to helm the recording. From the start, one can hear the band isn't quite the same. The luminescent majesty is there, but the pace is relatively ponderous, and the orchestrated results aren't blended in as organically as intended. *Visions of the Emerald Beyond* (1975) begins strongly with the two-part "Eternity's Breath," a massive slice of cosmic prog with celestial group vocals, but the rest is unfocused, veering from dirty funk to pastoral folk to spacey ballads from one short track to the next. *Inner Worlds* (1976), with its off-putting cover featuring a close-up of a shirtless McLaughlin, was a limp finish to the Mahavishnu saga, with scattered keyboards, indistinct grooves, and a blandness previously unthinkable. McLaughlin hardly surprised anyone when he retired the Mahavishnu Orchestra enterprise soon after.

McLaughlin's next choice was a complete surprise: He left his discipleship with Sri Chinmoy. He still followed the teachings, felt grateful for the development of his inner life, but wanted to take charge of his own actions.[29] The most public of those actions was to form a new band with only Indian musicians, named Shakti, after the divine energy force in Hinduism. McLaughlin had met famed tabla player Zakir Hussain years earlier, and the two added L. Shankar on violin, plus percussionists Vikku Vinayakram and Ramnad Rhagavan. Shakti recorded three excellent albums over the next two years, but the diamond is the debut, simply called *Shakti with John McLaughlin* (1976). Recorded live on July 5, 1975, at Southampton College on Long Island, the album is acoustic, but with the explosiveness and speed of the Mahavishnu Orchestra, especially on side two's single track that bursts with intensity and spirituality over a full half hour: "What Need Have I For This—What Need Have I For That—I Am Dancing At The Feet Of My Lord—All Is Bliss—All Is Bliss." Perhaps the greatest song title in all of 1970s jazz fusion, it's also one of McLaughlin's crowning achievements.

Refreshed by his Shakti sojourn, McLaughlin finished off the 1970s by making the choice not to join or form any band at all. He resumed his solo career with *Electric Guitarist* (1978), which hosted an overflowing bevy of fusion friends, including some of his former Mahavishnu bandmates, Chick Corea, Patrice Rushen, and even his old Lifetime pals Jack Bruce and Tony Williams. The follow-up, *Electric Dreams* (1979), featured a more settled band, which now included Shakti's L. Shankar on violin. Both are highly enjoyable and successfully reincorporate jazz vibes into the mix, but they lack those blazing moments that had become McLaughlin's trademark.

In the decades since, McLaughlin has made many wonderful records, especially the acoustic guitar trio albums he made with flamenco star Paco de Lucía and Return to Forever's Al Di Meola. He reunited with Shakti for a couple of albums; formed the short-lived, fusion-styled Five Peace Band with Chick Corea; and by 2010 was releasing albums with his regular backing band, the 4th Dimension. He has explored various genres (Brazilian music, electronica, acid jazz, etc.), and he still plays with that hard, fast, intense technique and tone. In every case, though, he has sounded more relaxed than he ever did in the 1970s. He sounds like one who has flown into the sun and come out the other side with the knowledge, but without the pressure anymore to be a musical and spiritual prophet. A beatific smile continued to grace his face as he greeted his fans online for New Year's 2018: "We are One, we have always been One, we can only be One."[30]

*****

Up until his death from cancer in 2021, Chick Corea spent his whole life as a restless musician, ranging from the brashly avant-garde to the brazenly commercial, and spent the decades since the 1970s recording dozens of acoustic and electric albums with colleagues new and old. One of his most symbolic musical reunions was with Herbie Hancock. Back in 1968, Miles Davis admired Corea's loud, percussive way of playing chords and abruptly chose him to replace Hancock in his band. Despite Miles's decision, Corea and Hancock always appreciated each other's adventurous artistry, then and thereafter. So they toured as a piano duo in 1978, releasing a pair of double live albums in the process, and did so again in 2015, just two genius veterans and their keyboards.[31]

Corea always credited Miles's fateful invitation to a simple intervention by a mutual friend: Tony Williams. "Tony was a Boston friend of mine, and we had played together before Tony moved out of Boston into New York," Corea remembered in 2003. "At the time when Herbie was leaving the band, Tony recommended me to Miles and it was simple as that, that's how I began to play."[32] And so, as always and once again throughout jazz history, adventurous artists advanced the music. And when they made a loud enough splash, they created virtuous circles that rippled and overlapped each other.

Long before he stirred the waters of jazz fusion, Armando Anthony Corea was born on June 12, 1941, in Chelsea, Massachusetts. Thanks to an aunt who called him "Cheeky" because she loved pinching his young face, Armando was soon and thereafter known as "Chick." His father was a trumpeter, so Corea was surrounded by music from a young age, playing piano by the age of four.[33] He also played the single-valve bugle[34] in the local St. Rose Scarlet Lancers Drum and Bugle Corps. After graduating from nearby Everett High School in 1959,[35] he went to New York for college, studying at Columbia before transferring to Juilliard, where—like his future mentor, Miles—he dropped out to dive into a career as a professional jazz musician.[36] Soon enough, he earned prestigious gigs playing behind Dizzy Gillespie, big-band singer Cab Calloway, and singer Sarah Vaughan. By the end of the 1960s, he was drawn to the sound and the volume of electric keyboards, which led to his two years of adventurous sonic journeys in Miles Davis's band. And he was there when the iconic trumpeter played his largest-ever concert in front of 600,000 people at the Isle of Wight music festival.

But Corea was too interested in creating his own music to stay in Miles's orbit for long. Corea began his post-Miles career by fully embracing free jazz and abstract composition with the group Circle, whose other members included bassist Dave Holland, drummer Barry Altschul, and Anthony Braxton. He then joined up with the German record label ECM for two volumes of *Piano Improvisations* (1971, 1972), stunning solo albums that formed a bridge between his atonal experiments and the heartwarming melodic lyricism that came with his next major career shift.

Corea decided to form a far more accessible band than Circle, so he recruited Stanley Clarke on bass, Joe Farrell on soprano sax and flute, Brazilian percussionist Airto Moreira, and Moreira's wife, Flora Purim, on vocals and percussion. By this point, Corea had embraced Scientology and become a lifelong acolyte of *Dianetics* author L. Ron Hubbard, so he called the band Return to Forever, which carried a strong whiff of sci-fi mysticism. "Forever is a word which means a duration of time without ending, you see," Corea explained to jazz writer Les Tomkins in 1972,

> and it implies a place where people are when they're not thinking about time, not embroiled in the world, and they're very much themselves. Where time just passes without being noticed. And it's a very beautiful place to be; it's a very light, happy place, where a lot of production and creativity happens. It's not really a place or a time; it's just a way of being, and it's a return to that, you see.[37]

When the album *Return to Forever* came out in 1972, it was indeed beautiful, light, and happy—sometimes so blissfully ethereal that the flutes, vocals, and Corea's electric piano left the gentle polyrhythms behind.

The sound was so appealing that the same year Corea, Clark, and Moreira joined Tony Williams in backing bossa nova sax legend Stan Getz of "Girl From Ipanema" fame, both on live dates and on his album *Captain Marvel*. A delightful record and one that updated Getz's sound for the fusion era, it also featured compositions by Corea that would appear on Return to Forever's next album, *Light as a Feather* (1973). The group's sophomore effort has a more immediate sound than its predecessor and boasts epic classics like the title track and "Spain," which would become Corea's signature tune for decades to come. Indeed, it's a graceful record that seamlessly fuses jazz, electric instruments, and Latin rhythm, but despite its artistic success, Moreira, Purim, and Farrell split from this first version of the band by early 1973.

The second Return to Forever is the incarnation that most people remember, in large part because here Corea & Co. fully embraced jazz-rock. Bassist Clarke became as revered as Weather Report's Jaco Pastorius or the Headhunters' Paul Jackson, as his dexterity and versatility delivered a powerful bottom end to heavy riffs or funkified a tune to booty-shaking nirvana. His rhythm section partner was Lenny White—yet another *Bitches Brew* alumnus—who had the power and groove to rival Mahavishnu's Billy Cobham. And on guitar, Return to Forever had Bill Connors splashing hot licks all over *Hymn of the Seventh Galaxy* (1973), an album so proudly bombastic that it was thrilling for their many fans but divisive for critics. Now seen as a jazz-rock landmark, the album confounded Robert Christgau, who wrote: "The futuristic, Mahavishnu-style jazz-rock gets hot enough at times to make you believe in spirit energy. But Corea's themes lack the grandeur of McLaughlin's, and what good is God without grandeur?"[38]

Regardless, Return to Forever started playing the same concert hall circuit as McLaughlin, Hancock, and Weather Report. They didn't miss a beat when Connors left after one album, replacing him with a young Al Di Meola, a flashy young Berklee grad who was extraordinarily fast on the guitar and could switch between jazz, rock, and even flamenco as needed. Clarke and White amped up the funk quotient, and Corea was now playing synthesizers with the melodic ease of Joe Zawinul, albeit at twice the speed. Together this lineup recorded three albums: *Where Have I Known You Before* (1974), which managed to sound both expansive and hectic; the Grammy-winning[39] *No Mystery* (1975), which has the grand distinction of sounding like Sly and the Family Stone playing danceable electronic prog; and *Romantic Warrior* (1976), which refined the bewildering fireworks of the previous records into a more polished approach, reintroduced some jazz piano among the synths, and funneled it all through a bizarre medieval concept. Whether or not these albums were in good or bad taste, they were glittery and giddy.

Audiences certainly agreed: By the end of this run, Return to Forever was packing those halls and landing albums on the *Billboard* pop, jazz, and R&B charts. But this version of Return to Forever eventually imploded too, replaced by a third version with an expanded horn section that left behind one shockingly bland studio album, *Musicmagic* (1977), and a bloated triple live album. It was almost like Return to Forever had been a spectacular Day-Glo-frosted cake of so many tiers and sparkling candles that it was destined to tip over and fall flat at some point.

Even if Return to Forever was Corea's highest profile gig in the 1970s, he also made a series of fusion solo records, which sound garish one moment and sublime the next. The best are *The Leprechaun* (1976) and the double album *My Spanish Heart* (1976), in part because they feature ample amounts of Corea's lovely acoustic piano and Latin rhythms to balance out the over-the-top use of synths and horns. Ironically, some of the best music he made arrived on the duet albums he recorded with vibraphonist Gary Burton for the ECM label, especially 1973's *Crystal Silence*. Over nine tracks, this album glistens with gorgeous, twinkling sound, and it's so magical, one can return to this album forever. It's also testimony that Corea could be loud and brash like his contemporaries, but he could achieve more sublime visions by being quiet and mellow.

Ten Essential 1970s Jazz Fusion Albums by Three Loud Visionaries

Emergency!, by The Tony Williams Lifetime (1969)
Turn It Over, by The Tony Williams Lifetime (1970)
The Inner Mounting Flame, by Mahavishnu Orchestra (1971)
Return to Forever, by Chick Corea (1972)
Birds of Fire, by Mahavishnu Orchestra (1973)
Crystal Silence, by Chick Corea & Gary Burton (1973)
Light as a Feather, by Chick Corea and Return to Forever (1973)

Love Devotion Surrender, by Carlos Santana and Mahavishnu John McLaughlin (1973)
No Mystery, by Return to Forever, featuring Chick Corea (1975)
Shakti with John McLaughlin, by Shakti (1976)

5 Ten Crossover Virtuosos
Freddie Hubbard, Donald Byrd, Patrice Rushen, George Benson, Grover Washington Jr., and More

Perhaps you heard it back in 1978, when it was ubiquitous on every radio station and reached No. 4 on the Billboard Hot 100. Perhaps you heard it decades later, used as a musical punchline on animated sitcoms like *King of the Hill*[1] or *South Park*.[2] Perhaps you're hearing it in a supermarket right now as you shop for groceries. With its familiar flugelhorn melody and bouncy bass, you know this song. *Everyone* knows this song. Wherever or whenever, it's possibly the most recognizable theme in jazz fusion, and even the most hardened cynic can't help but have their mood lift when they hear it. Quite appropriately, it's called "Feels So Good" by Chuck Mangione.

The massive hit made Chuck Mangione an instantly recognizable name, and the *Feels So Good* album cover made him an instantly recognizable face, with his long hair, bearded smile, and a felt porkpie hat—so iconic that he donated it to the

Smithsonian's National Museum of American History.[3] But he also suffered fierce backlash from the jazzerati, who regarded him as a mercenary flash in the pan, happy to make bank from easy listening. In fact, Mangione was already a veteran of the jazz world, a graduate from the prestigious Eastman School of Music who spent the 1960s playing with Art Blakey's Jazz Messengers, following in the footsteps of revered trumpet players Freddie Hubbard and Lee Morgan.[4]

But none of that mattered to the critics who called him "Chuck Mediocre" at the height of his fame, to which Mangione replied in a 1979 *Washington Post* interview: "Our music is very accessible. I don't want to play anything that people have to use a dictionary to understand... I always tried to play melodic music. I'm here to play the kind of music I like. And I'm very grateful that the public has accepted my music."[5] Despite the skepticism of this melodic style, Mangione was merely the highest charting example of this kind of jazz fusion that didn't seek to blow you away with power or blow your mind with innovation, but rather the kind of jazz fusion that was simply *pleasurable* if you just let it play.

*****

Freddie Hubbard was the finest trumpeter of his generation, a worthy successor to Miles Davis, with his ability to deliver lightning-fast blowouts or gently intoned ballads. A genuinely exciting musician, he filled out his 1960s with a series of excellent Blue Note albums of his own while working as a favorite sideman to icons and rising stars like Wes Montgomery, Herbie Hancock, Wayne Shorter, and Quincy Jones. Hubbard was also the only musician to perform on all three of the

1960s most foundational avant-garde jazz albums—Ornette Coleman's revolutionary *Free Jazz* (1961), Eric Dolphy's abstract *Out To Lunch!* (1964), and John Coltrane's collective-improv freakout, *Ascension* (1966). Nobody, ever, would dare call him mediocre.

Then in May 1970, he released *Red Clay*, barely more than a month after Miles Davis's *Bitches Brew*, and helped usher jazz fusion into different direction. Whereas *Bitches Brew* inspired a generation to add rock elements and studio experimentation, *Red Clay* inspired other artists to incorporate seriously funky bass, drums, and electric piano—played here by Miles alums Ron Carter, Lenny White, and Herbie Hancock, respectively—into a soulful stew that made you get down and move, even as Hubbard and saxophonist Joe Henderson took virtuosic jazz solos. Years later, Hubbard would tell journalist Scott Yanow that this was one of the favorite fusion albums he made:

> When I'm playing it, I have more of a feeling, because that's my roots. But most of the guys in my group are younger and don't know anything about playing with Miles or Sonny Rollins or Bud Powell. I have to try to explain it to them. I found that mixing it up a little bit, combining my music with the so-called music of today, it becomes more understandable to them.[6]

Hubbard perfected this approach on *Red Clay*, and on other irresistible albums he recorded for producer Creed Taylor's new CTI label, such as *Straight Life* (1971), *First Light* (1971), and *Sky Dive* (1973). These albums brought Hubbard increased commercial success and a record deal with Columbia, but his lush, funky formula in the late 1970s became consistently inconsistent. For every awkward clunker, like his bizarre cover of Gary Wright's soft-rock hit "Dream Weaver" on *Windjammer* (1976), there was at least one masterpiece, such as "Little Sunflower" on *The Love Connection* (1979)—a shimmering nine-minute fever dream with mesmerizing vocals by Al Jarreau. He ended up losing the good will of critics, who couldn't understand how such an adventurous musician could embrace such a crass direction. Hubbard responded that he was still adventurous, but in a pragmatic way. "It's hard to survive playing just straight-ahead," he explained to the *Los Angeles Times* in 1988. "Sometimes I want to do a little of everything, from working with radio orchestras in Europe to making commercials and funk records. I like to do different things, not only for the money but partly because I know I can do it."[7]

Hubbard was not the only veteran trumpeter scoring big in the 1970s with jazz-funk. If all Donald Byrd had done in life was discover Herbie Hancock in 1960, bringing the young pianist to New York, he would have made a major contribution to jazz and jazz fusion. But even at that point, Byrd was an important figure in jazz, both onstage and off. An exceptionally learned man, Byrd earned a bachelor's degree in music from Wayne State University and a master's degree from the Manhattan School of Music. He also believed strongly in educating others, so that even in the 1960s, when he was a prolific hard-bop recording artist for Blue Note, he was teaching at New York's High School of Music & Art. Soon he moved up to teaching at universities, such as Rutgers, Hampton, and Delaware State. At Howard University, he not only founded the jazz department but was later named the chair of the Black Music Department. By the time this remarkable scholar was through, he had earned six degrees over his lifetime, including a PhD and a law degree.[8] Known as "the Professor," he also made a host of hit records.

Byrd's first notable foray into bringing soul directly into jazz came with *A New Perspective* (1964), where he merged a standard jazz quintet with electric guitar, vibes, and a jazzy gospel choir. His music radiated deep soul, and it was a smooth but gradual transition into soulful fusion in 1970, when the evocative and atmospheric *Electric Byrd* went deep into space blues à la *Bitches Brew*, and when *Ethiopian Knights* (1972) explored a grittier, earthier sound. These incremental changes led up to *Black Byrd* (1973), with its full-on funky soul delivered with a summery joy that makes you almost dizzy as you dance. The title track is the killer, with wah-wah rhythm guitar, a mammoth bassline, and group vocals singing about the superhuman musician as if he's some action hero—even Blue Note historian Richard Havers pithily describes the whole album as "Isaac Hayes' soundtrack to *Shaft* with stronger jazz overtones."[9] A massive hit that topped the jazz and R&B charts, *Black Byrd* also surged up the pop charts and sold more than 300,000 copies in its first year, ten times more than a typical Blue Note success.[10]

Black Byrd hit such R&B highs in large part because it was the trumpeter's first collaboration with the brothers Larry and Alphonso "Fonce" Mizell, Motown record producers and songwriters who helped create the Jackson 5's signature hits "I Want You Back" and "ABC."[11] Together, Byrd and the Mizells made a series of engagingly warm and bright albums throughout the 1970s, with *Street Lady* (1973) and *Places And Spaces* (1975) particularly standing out. Of course, hidebound critics disliked how his hits affected jazz, which in turn affected Byrd, as he recalled in 1982: "They had a feast on me for 10 years: 'He's sold out.' Everything that's bad was attributed to Donald Byrd."[12] But the trumpeter had the last word with his massive legacy. In addition to the jazz programs he launched in higher education, the Professor also taught generations of musicians, and once hip-hop discovered his 1970s music, he was sampled on hundreds of songs by seminal artists like Nas, A Tribe Called Quest, Pete Rock & C.L. Smooth, 2Pac, De La Soul, J Dilla, and so many more.[13] In 2000, the National Endowment of the Arts granted Byrd the ultimate honorific of "Jazz Master,"[14] but he had earned that title long ago, purists be damned.

At the same time that the Mizells were making the Professor an R&B legend, they made soul-jazz masterpieces with a young flautist named Bobbi Humphrey. Raised in Dallas, Humphrey picked up the instrument in ninth grade, which helped her get a college scholarship, and soon after graduating from Southern Methodist University, she won competitions at Harlem's Apollo Theatre.[15] As the first woman instrumentalist signed to Blue Note,[16] Humphrey joined forces with the Mizells for her third album, the stone-classic *Blacks and Blues* (1973), with cinematic urban-soul epics like "Chicago, Damn" and "Harlem River Drive." This album of swaying grooves lent itself to Humphrey's gorgeous melodic sense and dexterity, and it's fair to say that she reconceptualized the flute with this record.

Humphrey continued in the same vibrant vein with the Mizells on *Satin Doll* (1974) and *Fancy Dancer* (1975), both as wonderful as *Blacks and Blues*. Then she moved on to work with R&B veterans like Skip Scarborough, who had crafted hits with Bill Withers and Earth, Wind & Fire, and Ralph McDonald, who did the same with Roberta Flack and Grover Washington Jr. Though her recorded output is rather scant compared to her prolific peers, she too looms large over contemporary music: Her music remains a staple for DJ lounge sessions,[17] as well as a hip-hop source for artists ranging from DJ Jazzy Jeff & the Fresh Prince to Wiz Khalifa.[18] And she embraced playing live, whether in clubs for enraptured audiences or at home to enrapture herself. "I play my flute every morning on my porch," she told *New York Amsterdam News* in 2016. "The birds respond to my rhythmic patterns. I try to create something every day."[19] And if there's a better statement expressing the quotidian joy of jazz, it has yet to be said.

*****

Growing up in Panama in the 1940s, Billy Cobham was raised by a piano-playing father and lived among cousins who played steel drums and timbales for money. Thanks to Carnival season, he grew up with a love of percussion, marching music, and parades. He moved to New York as a child and, much like Tony Williams, he was a self-taught drummer whose first inspiration came from following his dad to club gigs.[20] As a teen, he played drums at the High School of Music & Art,[21] where Donald Byrd would teach, before spending three years in the US Army Band. By 1968, he was backing hard-bop pianist Horace Silver, and all these influences in his life clicked into his trademark style of massive power paired with uncanny precision. "My experiences as a musician, the military bands, the funk," he mused in 2014, "it's all in there."[22]

Cobham was an early pioneer of jazz fusion drumming, cofounding the short-lived fusion group Dreams in the late 1960s, which is remembered now because members included future stars like him, guitarist John Abercrombie, and the Brecker Brothers on horns. He also was a sought-after session drummer, working with soul-jazz artists on CTI Records and with Miles Davis on electric albums like *A Tribute to Jack Johnson*. On that album, he played alongside guitarist John McLaughlin, who recruited him for the fiercely spiritual Mahavishnu Orchestra. Cobham was now a star himself, and when that band broke up, he recorded his first solo album, the crucial fusion masterpiece *Spectrum* (1973). Most of the tracks were based on the thunderous rumblings of Cobham's drums and the lightning-fast pianos and synths of Mahavishnu's Jan Hammer. Aggressive yet loose, it's an ideal blend of jazz-rock and jazz-funk that still resurfaces decades later in tunes like Massive Attack's trip-hop classic "Safe From Harm," which lifted its throbbing bassline wholesale from *Spectrum*'s centerpiece, "Stratus."[23]

The remainder of Cobham's albums in the 1970s maintained the same blend of synths, bass, guitars, and horns, all funking as hard and as fast as they can to keep up with the dynamo behind the drum kit. If they're not always as individually distinctive as the dreamy *Crosswinds* or the densely bouncy *Total Eclipse* (both 1974), they're certainly great fun to blast at a barbecue or on headphones while out on a morning run. As catholic in his musical outlook as Tony Williams, Cobham recorded not only dozens of his own varied albums but also dozens more backing up jazz legends like Gil Evans and rock heroes like Peter Gabriel. His biggest honor came in 2024, when the Panama Jazz Festival dedicated its twenty-first edition to its headliner, the country's famous jazz native son. "As a person born in Coco Solo Hospital in Colón, Panama," Cobham reflected, "I never dreamed that I would have the opportunity to perform in front of my countrymen and women at 80 years of age . . . It is more than an honor for me to be presented in such a special place."[24]

Among the many bands Cobham joined, few were as fun and funky as the one he formed with keyboardist George Duke. Perhaps that's because few jazz fusion artists were as fun and funky as Duke himself, a congenial teddy bear of a man then known for his jokey personality in Frank Zappa's backing band. The Billy Cobham-George Duke Band toured for only a year and released only the album *"Live" on Tour in Europe* (1976), based on raucous gigs in Montreux, Switzerland, and London.[25] But its success finally gave Duke the status to permanently establish himself as a major-label solo artist.

Duke made a name for himself years before in the Bay Area, getting his bachelor's degree from the San Francisco Conservatory of Music, then a master's degree from San Francisco State, starting a jazz group with singer Al Jarreau, and releasing a series of bouncy albums on small independent labels. He also formed a trio with jazz violinist Jean-Luc Ponty that gained him such renown that he was soon recruited to join Joe Zawinul's former boss, saxman Cannonball Adderley, and then Zappa at his jazz-rock height.[26]

Once he was on his own on a major label, he enjoyed the expensive budgets for recording, distribution, and promotion, and it all coalesced on his massive success, *Reach for It* (1977). Here the tunes are shorter, tighter, and swing like mad, whether burning with rock guitars, percussion whirlwinds from Leon "Ndugu" Chancler and Weather Report's Manolo

Badrena, or bouncing in a P-Funk style with the wiggly bass of Byron Miller. *Reach for It* ended up being Duke's biggest hit, spending six months on the Billboard pop chart, where it peaked at No. 25.[27] More importantly, the album hit No. 4 on the R&B chart,[28] as Duke closed out the 1970s as a star of funk rather than jazz. In the 1980s and 1990s, his albums updated jazz with a smooth sheen and new jack swing rhythms, and Duke became a sonic touchstone for hip-hop artists like Common, electronic titans like Daft Punk, and sui generis souls like bassist-singer Thundercat, who combines all these genres. For Duke, it was just a result of lessons learned from listening to jazz fusion's Promethean leader. "Miles taught me how to play a melody, how to play the spaces, how to move between diverse styles of music," Duke explained to the UK jazz website Just Soul in 2006. "He taught me that it was possible for a musician to look deep inside and play the music of his heart without compromise, and still be a star!"[29]

In the same interview, Duke also cited Les McCann as one of his first influences, thanks to his ability to evoke a gospel vibe in even the most secular settings. Born in Kentucky in 1935, the self-taught McCann was a seasoned veteran by the time he hit it big at the end of the 1960s. Over the course of that decade, McCann was based on the West Coast, and he brought his soulful style to more than a dozen albums recorded for the Pacific Jazz label, under his own name and in collaboration with labelmates like the Jazz Crusaders and Richard "Groove" Holmes. He may have been Pacific Jazz's best-selling artist at the time,[30] but his big break came when he jumped over to Ahmet Ertegun's R&B mecca, Atlantic Records.

Recorded at the 1969 Montreux Jazz Festival with tenor saxman Eddie Harris, *Swiss Movement* was a masterpiece of God-given grooves, driven by McCann's effusive piano playing that sounds like he's tearing the roof off a gospel revival. The highlight is the protest song "Compared to What." Although it has been recorded by many artists, only McCann's eight-minute live version has achieved the status of eternal soul-jazz standard. The explosive rhythm section of bassist Leroy Vinnegar and Donald Dean drives the song forward as McCann sings trenchant lyrics about the chaos and hypocrisy of the Vietnam War era. Eminently enjoyable, the album topped the *Billboard* jazz chart and hit the upper echelons of the R&B and Billboard pop charts, earning a Grammy nomination along the way.[31]

By the early 1970s, McCann embraced electronics, enabling him to create a stratospheric synthesizer symphony called *Layers* (1973). Aside from a base of acoustic congas, blocks, and bells, he played the entire opus, even sending the drummers home so he could experiment with various keyboards, especially the sound-sculpting ARP synthesizer. "I had the feeling that the instruments were alive," McCann rhapsodized in the album's liner notes. "It was like magic—magic from childhood—magic for now—and magic for all time. It wasn't only that first night that I became the whole orchestra and all the music, I went back night after night. So what you hear is actually one continuous song."[32] In fact, McCann created so many tracks and such dense sound that engineer Robert Litfin had to link together two sixteen-track machines to mix them all;[33] as a result, *Layers* is often credited as music's first thirty-two-track recording. Unsurprisingly for such a bold record, it divided critics then and now. Some felt the technology was too overwhelming, while others thought the music was mind-blowing, saying that "McCann sounds like he was in touch with another dimension."[34] With the music's warmth and humanity miraculously forged from machines, *Layers* is a self-contained reverie of McCann's memories and emotions, and it's one with an uncannily synesthetic affect, evoking the vivid hues of sunsets, the flair of school marching bands, and the sticky air of summer nights in the neighborhood. There is really no other album like it in this book.

Months before McCann layered his magnum synth opus in the fall of 1972, Patrice Rushen was a senior at Los Angeles's Alain Leroy Locke High School, created in the late 1960s as a safe center of learning for Black teens. She wasn't just any senior, but a piano prodigy whose groups won the Battle of the Bands at the Hollywood Bowl and the All-Star High School competition at the Monterey Jazz Festival.[35] She then enrolled at the University of Southern California, and while she was completing her double major in music education and piano performance,[36] she also earned a reputation as a fresh young jazz talent who could master any keyboard or genre. Her confident debut album, *Prelusion* (1974), came out when she was just twenty years old. It's mostly a straightforward jazz release until the final track, "Puttered Bopcorn," a *Layers*-esque tune where Rushen overdubs swooping ARP synthesizer tones over percolating clavinet and electric piano. From then on, Rushen leaned hard into electronic jazz-funk albums, collaborating with other masters of the genre as Headhunters percussionist Bill Summers and Earth, Wind & Fire guitarist Al McKay.

She could also sing, arranging vocals differently for each track—whether a light and sultry solo voice, a joyous P-Funk-style chorale, or robotic drawls through a vocoder. All of her early music was so catchy and danceable that she too moved to a major label, Elektra, and established herself as a mainstream R&B artist, albeit one who could lay down keyboard parts equal to either Herbie Hancock or Stevie Wonder. Her commercial breakthrough came with *Pizzazz* (1979), anchored by the smash hit disco classic "Haven't You Heard." On the surface, it sounds like she's completely abandoned jazz, but once the instrumental breaks bubble over with horns and keyboard solos, *Pizzazz* reveals itself as a more complex, brilliant record on its own terms. "Blacks have always danced and they always will—right back to the big band and jazz sound of the '20's and '30's, then right on through R&B and pop," Rushen explained to *Blues & Soul* in 1980. "Today, there is far more of a Black influence on pop music than there has ever been . . . To me, the whole album is just a mixture of what we call jazz fusion and R&B dance music."[37]

Thanks to her continued success, Rushen has been able to set her own terms ever since. She is best known for her song "Forget Me Nots," which was an international chart smash across all genres in 1982, and then again in 1997 when rapper-turned-actor superstar Will Smith recast the entire song as "Men in Black," the monster hit from the movie of the same name. She's worked on records by pop stars like Prince and Boyz II Men, but also ones by jazz legends like Lionel Hampton and Nancy Wilson. And as if jazz, fusion, R&B, and funk weren't enough, Rushen was the Detroit Symphony Orchestra's composer-in-residence for the 2000–2001 season. Then in 2013, she went back to her alma mater, USC, this time as a professor and chair of its popular music program.[38] And the spirit of her jazz fusion generation in the 1970s inspired it all. As she told the electronic-dance publication *Mixmag* in 2022: "We were hybrids that came from a generation that gave us permission to go for whatever we wanted musically, as long as it was presented at a high level, creating an environment that told us it's okay to do our thing, because we were already standing on the shoulders of those who have done it." And she was pleased to offer her shoulders to the next generation of genre-bending musicians. "That's the way it's supposed to go."[39]

*****

Few musicians in jazz history have been as handsome and debonair as George Benson. At the same time, few people in jazz history have been able to play guitar like George Benson, with his blend of funky fire and silky soul. As a result, few people in jazz history have had the same consistent level of success decade after decade, which is why it's heartwarming to learn that his first professional gig came when he was just seven years old, playing ukelele at a corner drug store in Pittsburgh's Hill District. Benson's home neighborhood was the heart of Black culture in the city, so within a year, the precocious boy guitarist had moved up to playing in a local unlicensed nightclub on weekends. By 1954, ten-year-old "Little Georgie"—as he was known—recorded his first single, "She Makes Me Mad,"[40] a swinging tune spiritedly sung by a boy whose voice has yet to drop.[41] Heard today, it's adorable.

Exactly ten years later, Benson recorded *The New Boss Guitar of George Benson*, his first solo album, and here his adorable singing has given way to absolute fluidity on the guitar, as he could play fast solos, groovy rhythm, and bent strings with a graceful ease. In 1968, he became the first electric guitarist to record with Miles Davis, on the album *Miles in the Sky*, and soon after became one of the marquee artists on CTI Records. There he recorded albums like the bluesy *Beyond the Blue Horizon* (1971) and the boogie-ing *Body Talk* (1973) that are supremely atmospheric, whether played at night with the lights down low or in the full morning sun the day after.

His 1976 debut for Warner Bros lifted him to a whole new level. *Breezin'* arrived on the airy wings of its title track, whose melodic theme and lush string arrangements by Claus Ogerman made it a radio staple, almost as instantly recognizable as Chuck Mangione's "Feels So Good." Benson's singing took center stage on this album as well, scatting in perfect unison with his guitar leads and belting out songs in an achingly rich voice that sounded eerily like Stevie Wonder. A stunningly sleek album, *Breezin'* went triple platinum[42] and rocketed to No. 1 on the Billboard pop chart and the R&B chart.[43] For some, Benson was veering too close to easy listening with these "clichéd, sugary songs of his fusion records,"[44] but the millions of music fans who bought the album disagreed, as did Benson. "I've come up against a lot of flack doing this album," Benson told *Sounds* in 1976.

> I wanted to get people into what we do through an R&B sense. My music is highly improvisational with very little unison. The object of the exercise was to reach a new audience without giving up the kind of musical air I need to move in. I need space to move around in . . . I'm trying to dwell honourably in

all of this. But I'm pretty excited myself. This is something I've worked on for a long time.[45]

As he strolled gracefully into 1980, he kicked off the new decade with another signature smash, "Give Me the Night," a disco classic with a slinky groove and lyrics about music in the air and lovin' everywhere. By July, it hit No. 4 on the Billboard Hot 100 and No. 1 on the R&B charts,[46] becoming the "Song of the Summer" long before that phrase became common pop-culture parlance. But as the weather got colder, a shimmering single by a different jazz fusion artist began to take its place,[47] one where saxman Grover Washington Jr. brought the jazz and singer Bill Withers brought the soul. With poetic words about crystal raindrops falling, rainbows in the mind, and how we can make it if we try, "Just the Two of Us" was a big hit then and has become a pop-culture touchstone for decades after.

"Just the Two of Us" was as buttery and beatific as anything by Benson or Mangione and as fun as anything by Duke or Rushen. But long before that iconic song, Washington also had a thriving career creating soulful jazz à la Hubbard or McCann and funking as hard as Cobham, Humphrey, and Byrd. Like just about everyone in this book, Washington began playing music as a child. Born in Buffalo, New York, in 1943, his first influence was his father, Grover Washington Sr., who played saxophone. Much like Benson, he was playing in clubs as a boy, hitting the town with his horn by the age of twelve.[48] By the time the 1970s came around, Washington was the prototypical journeyman: touring with R&B and jazz combos since he was sixteen, playing in the 19th Army Band at Fort Dix during a stint in the military, and then gigging all over New York and

Philadelphia, the latter of which he claimed as his home city from then on.[49] Thanks to a missing musician and a lucky break one afternoon in 1971, Washington began the path that made him a musical icon and a Philly hero.

Producer Creed Taylor had arranged a recording date for saxophonist Hank Crawford. However, when Crawford was unavailable because he had been arrested for marijuana possession, Taylor grabbed Washington, then a saxophonist in the backing horn section, and told him it was his session now. They recorded pop-music covers by the likes of the Gershwins, Marvin Gaye, and future collaborator Bill Withers. "As I was listening in the booth to Grover play, I knew immediately that he sounded great," Taylor said. "Hank was a blues master alto player, and Grover had a more lyrical, romantic thing going." That sound certainly worked for a wide audience, because when the album *Inner City Blues* came out in 1972, it was a crossover hit and even made a big fan out of Marvin Gaye himself.[50]

From thereon, Washington made a series of albums for Kudu, the subsidiary imprint of CTI Records, and they had the same celebratory sound as anything from Motown or Stax. By the time he recorded the ambitious double album *Soul Box* (1973), his repertoire mixed covers of Gaye, the Temptations, Stevie Wonder, and Billie Holiday, plus "Taurian Matador" from Billy Cobham's *Spectrum* album. Half the length but quadruple the success, *Mister Magic* (1975) is the first of the two albums that forever defined Washington's career. Beginning in deceptively bucolic fashion with bird songs and echoing Fender Rhodes, the album soon dives into four symphonic jams, each one with a deliberately different mood, from psychedelic funk to tender ballad to gutbucket stomp. He showcased the same emotional and instrumental versatility over the rest of the decade, even as his music gradually morphed into a consistent style of midtempo grooves and polished production.

And then came *Winelight* (1980), the second album that forever defined Washington's career. The cover image gives off a sophisticated air, with a golden glow lighting its reclining saxophone and glass of chardonnay. And the music within is just as suave, thanks to the elastic grooves from bassist Marcus Miller and drummer Steve Gadd and a glistening sheen from a team of keyboardists playing Fender Rhodes, clavinet, and the Oberheim 8-Voice synthesizer. Then there's the penultimate track, "Just the Two of Us." Some of its luster has taken on a weird patina since 1999, when the comedy film *Austin Powers: The Spy Who Shagged Me* featured a famous musical routine of the song by the goofy villains Dr. Evil and Mini-Me. By 2020, the song went viral on the social media app TikTok, with more than 700,000 people using it as a soundtrack for quirky thirty-second home videos.[51] However luscious or kitschy—depending on your taste—what makes the whole album excel is Washington's sax, wailing on solos that sound like a friend telling you a story.

Winelight has defined Washington's reputation for so long because this album and George Benson's *Breezin'* were so often given the credit—or the blame—for the slickly processed style that was dubbed "smooth jazz" in the 1980s. But it helped make jazz a commercially viable career for Washington, and it made him an icon in Philly, where a middle school is named after him, and where he towers over the streets around Temple University in a three-story mural. Despite these honors, he has often been unjustly omitted from surveys of jazz history, which bothered him later in life. "It hurts the jazz audience at large, because they don't get a complete picture of what the music is," he said in 1995, four years before he died from a sudden heart attack at just fifty-six. "There's a tendency to overintellectualize the music, but some things you just have to feel—that's where I'm coming from."[52] And where he was coming from was the noble, artistic motivation he shared with these other crossover virtuosos: the need to have just the two of us—both musician and listener—feel so good.

Ten Essential 1970s Jazz Fusion Albums by Ten Crossover Virtuosos

Red Clay, by Freddie Hubbard (1970)
Black Byrd, by Donald Byrd (1973)
Blacks and Blues, by Bobbi Humphrey (1973)
Layers, by Les McCann (1973)
Spectrum, by Billy Cobham (1973)
Mister Magic, by Grover Washington Jr. (1975)
Breezin', by George Benson (1976)
Feels So Good, by Chuck Mangione (1977)
Reach for It, by George Duke (1977)
Pizzazz, by Patrice Rushen (1979)

6 Two Pioneering Record Labels
CTI and ECM

With crossover success yielding packed concert halls and gold and platinum albums, jazz fusion was not only mainstream in the 1970s but also good business. By the end of the 1960s, faced with plummeting sales, Blue Note—the iconic jazz label par excellence—turned to jazz-funk and soon scored smash hits with releases by Donald Byrd and Bobbi Humphrey.[1] Major labels certainly noticed too, as they raided smaller labels and signed away young and old fusioneers, like Patrice Rushen and Freddie Hubbard. The most notable label was Columbia Records, which supported the lengthy careers of Miles Davis and Herbie Hancock and also introduced Weather Report and Mahavishnu Orchestra as arena-ready supergroups. "Partly due to the breakthroughs that Miles's albums had made, some people thought that jazz was going to be as big as rock'n'roll in the Seventies," wrote Clive Davis, Columbia's president from 1967 to 1973. "The rock audience was growing up and, as we've seen, growing more sophisticated in its tastes . . . so jazz seemed like a viable option for the generation that had come of age with rock'n'roll and was still looking for something new and exciting."[2] And that's exactly what record executive Creed Taylor was thinking with his boutique record label, Creed

Taylor Incorporated (CTI), which created a luxurious sound and vision, making every jazz fusion record an alluring object that could be enjoyed and collected, especially by aspiring adults looking to upgrade their lifestyle.

Growing up in rural Virginia in the 1930s and 1940s, Taylor told journalist Marc Myers in 2008 that he hated being surrounded by bluegrass and country music—literally, as the Carter Family lived two mountains away. Instead, he was drawn to the big-band jazz broadcasts he could catch on the radio. As a teenager, he was inspired by Harry James and Dizzy Gillespie to play trumpet in the high school band. Despite studying psychology at Duke University and serving in Korea with the US Marine Corps, he always had his goal set on moving to New York and getting involved with jazz.[3] In 1954, he hit the ground running in the Big Apple, landing a job at Bethlehem Records, then jumping up to ABC-Paramount, where he produced a wide variety of albums, from jazz to Latin, and developed his talents with orchestration.[4] By early 1960, he created a subsidiary for ABC that became one of the most iconic labels in jazz history: Impulse! Records. Though he didn't last long at Impulse!, he did produce the label's seminal early albums like Ray Charles's *Genius + Soul = Jazz*, Oliver Nelson's *Blues and the Abstract Truth*, and John Coltrane's *Africa/Brass*.

Along with such innovative music, his visual innovations in creating Impulse! indicated the approach he would take later with CTI. First off, he wanted a consistently recognizable design that was also eye-catching, whether filed on a bookshelf or displayed on a coffee table.[5] That meant a black-and-orange color palette on all the albums, which still make Impulse! albums stand out even today. Even more, it also meant laminated gatefold covers that looked "like lacquered furniture," he told *The Wall Street Journal* in 2011. "As a result, consumers would treat them better and leave them out at home for others to see."[6]

Taylor soon left for the established Verve label, and that is where he produced one of the most iconic jazz-pop songs of all time: the winsome "The Girl From Ipanema," sung by Astrud Gilberto and released on the Stan Getz/João Gilberto 1964 Grammy-winning[7] bestseller *Getz/Gilberto*. Here is where all of Taylor's talents come into play, from the breezy West Coast jazz sound to the warm Brazilian influence and the lovely, laminated gatefold album that paired perfectly with a tray of dry Manhattans served neat. From now on, Taylor was considered one of the top producers in any genre of music.

With such supreme cachet, Taylor launched CTI Records in 1967. Within his first year, he demonstrated his exquisite taste in talent, releasing early albums by up-and-coming artists like George Benson and Milton Nascimento and the final album by guitar hero Wes Montgomery. Whereas Impulse! had a trademark color scheme, CTI had a trademark photographer: Pete Turner. Turner had a recognizably bold style, mixing and matching surreal landscapes and intense close-ups, then rendering them in saturated color and hyperreal focus. The connection between the album titles, the cover images, and the music within was deliberately tenuous—Taylor would often just hint at a title, and Turner would dig deep into his rich photo archive[8]—but taken together, these elements made the album itself seem precious indeed. "We were creating a universal aesthetic that the world could enjoy and understand," Taylor wrote in a 2006 book of Turner's photographs.[9]

Along with Benson, Freddie Hubbard, and Grover Washington Jr., the musicians that Taylor recorded for CTI are a remarkable who's-who of generational talents. Like Hubbard, Stanley Turrentine and his tenor sax had been a staple on Blue Note throughout the 1960s, and he literally found his groove at CTI, whether on the soul-jazz classics *Sugar* (1970) and *Cherry* (1972) or on Brazilian-influenced albums like *Salt Song* (1971) and *Gilberto With Turrentine* (1971), his collaboration with the "Ipanema" chanteuse. The label increased its Brazilian quotient with three gorgeous gems recorded by the father of bossa nova, composer Antonio Carlos Jobim: *Wave* (1967), *Tide* (1970), and the sunset-soaked *Stone Flower* (1970), which sounds exactly like Pete Turner's cover photo of Jobim in silhouette as cigarette smoke wreathes his profile. Another Brazilian composer and arranger, Eumir Deodato, gave CTI the hit album *Prelude* (1973), a symphonic blend that swirls classical music into funk and jazz. Its signature song was a gloriously over-the-top cover of Richard Strauss's "Also Sprach Zarathustra"—best known as the theme of Stanley Kubrick's *2001: A Space Odyssey*—which miraculously hit No. 2 on the Billboard Hot 100 singles chart.[10]

Flautist Hubert Laws also embraced the classical side of jazz fusion. On the exquisitely serene *Afro-Classic* (1970) and his eclectic double album *In the Beginning* (1974), Laws plays affecting versions of Bach, Mozart, and Satie alongside soul-jazz originals, playful takes on Coltrane, and pop songs like James Taylor's "Fire and Rain." The best sample of CTI's all-stars is the *California Concert*, a live recording from a July 1971 Hollywood Palladium concert that convened Hubbard, Benson, Turrentine, Laws, Ron Carter, Billy Cobham, Airto Moreira, keyboardist Johnny Hammond, and alto saxman

Hank Crawford. With definitive live takes on Hubbard's "Red Clay" and Turrentine's "Sugar," one can still feel the heat from this distinctly smoldering night.

CTI's influence on jazz is divisive, however, as critics then and today have often dismissed this wealth of music as "scarcely provocative" easy listening.[11] Even a jazz-rock historian like Stuart Nicholson bemoaned how so many jazz geniuses succumbed to CTI's house style: "Despite the adventurous histories of its artists, the CTI label was a guarantee of smooth, listener-friendly jazz ... As safe for radio play as cocktail parties, Taylor had his artists record well-known melodies wherever possible to help sell their improvisational talents."[12] If you can hang up your hang-ups, however, the quality and joy of these albums remain undeniable. As jazz historian Ted Gioia aptly states, "[T]he mercantile motivations underpinning these albums rarely detracted from the music-making, and Taylor's efforts have mostly held up well with the passing years, largely due to the high caliber of the creative talents at play and the first-class production values involved."[13]

Unfortunately, CTI collapsed financially and went bankrupt in 1978,[14] leaving many golden discs out of print for years. The good news is that, over time, the label is being rediscovered by the hip-hop artists who have sampled CTI tracks; vinyl collectors thrilled to own these beautiful objects; and jazz newbies who can now stream this friendly music on their phones. By the time Taylor died in 2022 at age ninety-three, his greatest project was still reaching listeners and enhancing their lifestyles, just as he imagined in the 1970s.

*****

At the same time over in Munich, Germany, another record-label impresario was building a label around a vaunted stable of house musicians, atmospheric recordings, pristine production, and gorgeously evocative album covers. But whereas Taylor and CTI gave listeners the feeling of high society, Manfred Eicher and his Edition of Contemporary Music (ECM) record label gave listeners the feeling of high culture. The obvious difference is that CTI was proud to have its soul-jazz releases hit the charts, while ECM is proud of its refined avant-garde heritage, marketing itself with the slogan "the most beautiful sound next to silence." Even so, some of ECM's music in the 1970s could be very loud indeed.

Manfred Eicher founded ECM in 1969, just twenty-six years after he was born in the town of Lindau,[15] on the shores of Lake Constance in Bavaria. As a young man, he had a modest career as a jazz bassist and a promising career as a producer, having already worked for Deutsche Grammophon. He was driven to find a new way to present contemporary jazz, recording younger musicians who were expanding the art of improvisation. And the ECM name itself sounded less like a record company and more like a boutique book publisher, with an aim to treat each release as some carefully edited artistic statement.[16]

The label's first series of releases were arcane: the abstract piano of Paul Bley, the German freakout-rock of Wolfgang Dauner, and the free jazz improv by a young Chick Corea, fresh off his stint with Miles Davis. Other Miles alums, like bassist Dave Holland and keyboardist Keith Jarrett, soon became staples on the label, as did the broodingly intense saxophonist Jan Garbarek, who was instrumental in making ECM the top producer of innovative Scandinavian jazz. Eicher quickly proved himself a meticulous expert at recording these unique instrumentalists, such as the dulcet tones of Gary Burton's vibraphone and the swooping glissandos of Eberhard Weber's double bass. "Manfred Eicher embodies the ideal producer," Weber wrote in his 2015 memoir. "He has an excellent ear, hearing even 'fleas cough,' and also knows the technical details required to reach perfection. . . . You have to be absolutely sure of yourself, so it's advisable to appear in the studio fully prepared."[17]

Eicher cared just as much about how the albums looked, working with designers Barbara Wojirsch and Dieter Rehm, who were just as rigorous and meticulous about the ECM aesthetic of enigmatic, stark photography and clean, stylized typefaces. "Being impressed by the sheer quantity of things and messages day in and day out makes me want to remove as much as possible from my designs until only something essential, only a thought or a gesture, remains," said Wojirsch in a 1996 book that compiled all of ECM's album covers.[18] By then, they had achieved such a reputation for beauty and collectability that the tome was aptly called *Sleeves of Desire*.

If all of this sounds like quintessential European navel-gazing, perhaps it is. But it's no less savvy a marketing plan than Creed Taylor's, and once the label hit its stride in the early 1970s, the music was less ascetic and more revelatory, even ecstatic. Most famously, ECM has been the home for the solo piano improvisations of Keith Jarrett. This keyboard maestro first gained fame in Charles Lloyd's quartet that wowed the Monterey Jazz Festival in 1966, then dazzled in Miles Davis's electric band circa *Live-Evil*. After recording an ambitious fusion double album, *Expectations* (1972), on Columbia, Jarrett abandoned electricity for good.

Jarrett's trademark releases for ECM have been live albums, where he just sits down and plays extemporaneously for as long as it takes. Calling these concerts "spontaneous compositions," Jarrett performs in a dramatic range of genres, from jazz to gospel to avant-garde to folk melodies, and he does so in such a masterful way that—even without electricity—"Keith Jarrett solo piano" has become as unique a genre as "electric Miles." The releases are miraculous, such as the multimillion-selling[19] *The Köln Concert* (1975), perhaps ECM's most iconic recording; the wondrously gigantic 10-LP *The Sun Bear Concerts* (1978), the label's 100th release that even rock bible *Rolling Stone* called a "showstopper";[20] and the triple-LP *Solo Concerts: Bremen/Lausanne* (1973), which fuses all his styles and captures all his emotions in one of the greatest solo piano albums ever recorded. From a commercial and artistic standpoint, it's no exaggeration when critic Wolfgang Sandner writes that "Keith Jarrett is the most important jazz musician in the ECM catalogue."[21]

Hundreds of other musicians have made ECM their home, whether playing straight-ahead jazz, Afrocentric free jazz, or European chamber jazz. And jazz fusion thrived here as well, often thanks to familiar names. Chick Corea, for example, recorded his first Return to Forever album on ECM, while two of Herbie Hancock's colleagues went solo on the German label: Bennie Maupin's *Jewel in the Lotus* and Julian Priester's *Love, Love* (both 1974), which capture the spacy psychedelia of the Mwandishi band. After recording *Crystal Silence* (1973) with Corea, vibraphonist Gary Burton embarked on a long career on ECM, recording delicate acoustic duets with guitarist Ralph Towner on *Matchbook* (1975) and blurry soundscapes with his electric band on *Ring* (1974) and *Passengers* (1977). Weber played in Burton's group, as well as many other artists' ECM releases, but the double bassist had his own imperial phase throughout the 1970s. With his surreal, liquid intonation—only Jaco Pastorious could achieve a similar sound—Weber created albums of atmospheric fusion that weren't quite jazz or rock, but something new and magical. His 1974 debut, *The Colours of Chlöe*, positively shimmers with jazz elegance, a chorus of cellos, and ambient synthesizers. Enhanced visually by the vivid, naïve-art paintings by his wife, Maja, all his albums through the decade achieved an otherworldly daydream effect.

Even among all these eclectic sonic adventurers, ECM was also a welcome home for jazz-rock guitarists. One of the earliest to join was Norwegian axeman and Miles Davis fan Terje Rypdal, who bonded with Eicher over their mutual love of classical music and Elvis.[22] Like Weber, Rypdal shaded his albums with synthesizers, but here the lead instrument was a searing electric guitar tone that burned like Jimi Hendrix or Carlos Santana. *Odyssey* is his expansive masterwork from 1975, a double album that switches between nocturnal menace and a bucolic daze. It's a cinematic range that was also achieved by John Abercrombie, the guitarist who cofounded the short-lived jazz-rock group Dreams with Billy Cobham. In 1975, he formed the trio called Gateway with bassist Dave Holland and Jack DeJohnette, another alum of Charles Lloyd's and Miles Davis's bands. Gateway's self-titled album reached the volume of anything by John McLaughlin, but instead of achieving intensity with cosmic speed, Abercrombie used abstraction and pedal effects to create thrilling noise or acid-fried folk. He also fashioned gentle reveries on the guitar, especially on *Sargasso Sea* (1976), an album of duets with Ralph Towner. A cofounder of the New Age folk-jazz group Oregon, Towner could play whirlwinds of guitar parts on his trademark twelve-string, nowhere better than on *Solo Concert* (1980), which is as incantatory and mesmerizing as anything by Keith Jarrett.

And as the 1970s came to an end, a young guitarist named Pat Metheny emerged out of Gary Burton's band, impressing with his immaculate technique and an open-hearted but distant tone that evoked the Midwestern landscapes of his native Missouri. He recorded his serene first album, *Bright Size Life* (1976), with none other than superstar bassist Jaco Pastorius, then followed it up with Weber anchoring the bottom end on the aptly named *Watercolors* (1977). The guitarist then formed the Pat Metheny Group with Lyle Mays, a master of atmospheric keyboards, and together they recorded a series of jazz fusion albums for ECM that were distinctive for being brightly melodic and easy to enjoy without being easy listening. Their quintessential album of this period is *American Garage* (1979). From its sun-dappled opener, "Across The Heartland," to its twilit closer, "The Epic," the music is so eager and welcoming, it's a complete delight.

Like Jarrett, Metheny would become one of ECM's best-selling artists. But unlike the pianist, he moved on to a major label's bigger budget to create more elaborate studio productions. He had outgrown the aural simplicity of the most beautiful sound next to silence. "With Pat we made very good records and he became more and more successful," Eicher told the *Guardian* in 2010, "but then he told me that he had to have a different distributor and he wanted to produce his own ideas ... One has to accept that. It didn't hurt my feelings. I understood his needs."[23]

Of course, Eicher could be circumspect in the twenty-first century, because by then ECM had released many other top-selling albums and earned the iconic stature of other record labels like Blue Note, Impulse!, and Verve. But he was also affirming that the artists' needs come first, a priority and focus on integrity that he's maintained since the very beginning. Those artists have also long cherished another precious freedom: no pressure to sign long-term contracts.[24] They can come and go and pursue their own opportunities, with the option to stay if they'd like. "As a general rule, whoever joins with ECM stays with ECM," Weber wrote. "In spite of its global success, the label has remained a small business ... Everyone feels they are part of the whole, thinking with it, working with it, contributing to it."[25] The best example is Jarrett: Back when he joined the label in 1971, ECM's payroll consisted of just Eicher and an assistant,[26] and even as the pianist became world-renowned and top-selling, he remained with the label on the basis of a mere handshake.

Ten Essential 1970s Jazz Fusion Albums from Two Pioneering Labels

Stone Flower, by Antonio Carlos Jobim (1970, CTI)
Sugar, by Stanley Turrentine (1970, CTI)

California Concert: The Hollywood Palladium, by The CTI All-Stars (1972, CTI)
Prelude, by Deodato (1973, CTI)
In the Beginning, by Hubert Laws (1974, CTI)
Solo Concerts: Bremen/Lausanne, by Keith Jarrett (1973, ECM)
The Colours of Chlöe, by Eberhard Weber (1974, ECM)
Odyssey, by Terje Rypdal (1975, ECM)
Gateway, by Gateway (1975, ECM)
American Garage, by Pat Metheny (1979, ECM)

7 Ten Jazzbo Rockstars
Joni Mitchell, Earth, Wind & Fire, Frank Zappa, Santana, Steely Dan, and More

The story goes that Joni Mitchell first heard the miraculous bass of Jaco Pastorius on a mid-1970s road trip from LA to Maine. In Boulder, Colorado, she stopped in to visit guitarist Robben Ford, a member of her touring band who played on her most recent album, *The Hissing of Summer Lawns* (1975). Ford had an advance copy of Pastorius's debut album, and when the tender ballad "Portrait of Tracy" came on the stereo, Mitchell knew that she was hearing a musical innovator and an audacious kindred spirit. She was particularly wowed by Pastorius's trademark use of fluid melodies on the low end of the bass, highlighted by his chiming, pinging harmonics.[1] He had the charisma of someone comfortable calling himself the best bass player in the world, and thus was a good match for Mitchell, who was in her early thirties and already considered the greatest singer-songwriter in the world. "He had a big bushy ego that ruffled a lot of people," Mitchell recalled a decade later, "but even his arrogance appealed to me."[2] Together, they partnered on an exquisite series of albums that transformed her career through jazz fusion.

Mitchell was hardly a typical folk or pop star. Like many, she taught herself guitar as a teenager, but with her left hand weakened by a childhood case of polio, she couldn't play the fingerpicking patterns from her instructional records. So she threw them out and found her unique way around the frets.[3] Even back in the mid-1960s, when the Saskatchewan native was entering the folk scenes in New York and then LA, she was experimenting with what would be known as "Joni's weird chords," where she used alternative tunings on her guitar to create unusual voicings and droning sounds that enabled her to sound almost orchestral while playing solo.[4] Such unusual voicings gave added artistic depth to her earliest signature songs: "Both Sides Now" (1969's *Clouds*), "Big Yellow Taxi" (1970's *Ladies of the Canyon*), and "A Case of You" (1971's *Blue*). She made tentative forays into jazz tones on *For the Roses* (1972) with woodwind musician Tom Scott, who brought his whole fusion band, L.A. Express, to play on Mitchell's 1974 hit record, *Court and Spark*, and on a warm and loose live double album, *Miles of Aisles* (1974). By 1975, she felt confident enough to capture the drifting haze of LA society with *The Hissing of Summer Lawns*' jazzier, more experimental musical milieu.

Pastorius joined up on *Hejira* (1976), a sublime album whose impressionistic lyrics and open-vista sound evoke that meandering journey Mitchell made across North America the previous year. The very first track, "Coyote," sets the tone with its spare instrumentation: just subtle percussion, "Joni's weird chords," and Pastorius bubbling and chiming on the bass as if in conversation with Mitchell's tale of a wandering lothario.

If *Hejira* was cinematic like an intimate road movie, then the double album *Don Juan's Reckless Daughter* (1977) was the self-indulgent epic that can be later rediscovered as an ambitious work of genius.

For years, critics dismissed *Don Juan's Reckless Daughter* as a mess. To be fair, the biggest mess of Mitchell's career was the album cover, where she posed in Blackface as a sleazy male alter-ego she called "Art Nouveau."[5] In various interviews over the years, her explanations for this crassly racist image have been vague and confusing, and no matter what she could say, it remains a shocking choice for someone who was steeping herself in Black music traditions and becoming lifelong friends with Black jazz legends like Herbie Hancock and Wayne Shorter. Her egregious mistake was tacitly acknowledged when the album was remastered and reissued in 2024 with a new cover photograph of Joni as herself, grinning and obscured by a large yawping wolf's head.

As for the music, *Don Juan's Reckless Daughter* is mysterious and magical, unjustly misunderstood when it came out, as fans just wanted her to go back to her imperial phase of radio hits. *Rolling Stone*'s Janet Maslin led the way in 1978, saying that "[Mitchell] has been inexplicably inclined to let her music become shapeless as she tries to incorporate jazz and calypso rhythms that eventually overpower her . . . These days, she appears bent on repudiating her own flair for popular songwriting."[6] But the fiercely independent Mitchell was never the type to let anyone overpower her. Instead, she relished the new sui generis sounds she was making with Pastorius, jazz-funk singer Chaka Khan, percussionist Airto Moreira, Weather Report drummers Alex Acuña and Manolo Badrena, and

Wayne Shorter, who collaborated with her more in the years ahead. These artists help make Mitchell's more conventional songs sound otherworldly while also contributing to her expanding musical vision, including a sidelong jazz symphony called "Paprika Plains" and a drum-circle freakout called "The Tenth World." The whole album sounds like a heat mirage sprawling and flickering before a setting California sun. That inchoate magic draws you to its horizon the more you listen, but you have to take the time. Most people didn't, so it was her last album to go gold upon its release.[7]

Commercial success completely eluded her final "jazz" studio album, an homage and quasi-collaboration with legendary jazz bassist and composer Charles Mingus, who died in 1979, just months before the album came out. A stark, hermetic collection of spoken interludes and ghostly tunes, *Mingus* featured Mitchell hammering at her weird chords on her own songs or singing her lyrics based on Mingus's compositions, such as his elegiac standard "Goodbye Pork Pie Hat." Fittingly, only jazz musicians backed her on the record, including Herbie Hancock and three-quarters of Weather Report in Shorter, Pastorius, and drummer Peter Erskine. The reception from rock criticism's literati was predictably mixed, and Mitchell's days as a top 40 artist were pretty much over. Still, she finished out the 1970s—and her jazz phase—with her second live double album, the wonderful *Shadows and Light*, which was recorded in Santa Barbara in 1979. Mitchell and Pastorius collaborated with a new set of jazz fusion stars, including saxman Michael Brecker and guitarist Pat Metheny and his keyboardist Lyle Mays, all of whom bring a welcome brightness and openness to such enigmatic music.

Even if it managed to largely kill her album sales, Mitchell's jazz phase burnished her reputation as a brilliant musician, in addition to being a brilliant songwriter. But even though today she's lauded as a rock artist who excelled at incorporating jazz into her music, she always dismissed any suggestion that she was concerned with genre. "My songs . . . they're not folk music, they're not jazz, they're art songs," she explained at the Library of Congress in 2023, where she was honored with the prestigious Gershwin Award for Popular Song. "They embody classical things and jazzy things and folky things, long line poetry." But what about the bad reviews at the time? asked Librarian of Congress Carla Hayden. "[I'm] hard to discourage and hard to kill," said the legend, who had recently completed her recovery from a near-fatal brain aneurysm. And with that, the walls of the Library's Great Hall rumbled as the audience roared.[8]

*****

Mitchell became (and still is) the exemplar of the jazz-playing rock star, and the seeds of her artistic triumphs were first sown in the wild cultural winds of the late 1960s. Back then, Miles Davis and friends, of course, were forging fusion from a jazz perspective, but several rock and soul musicians were also joining in, and they were eager to fuse jazz with *their* music.

In 1967, Bronx-born nineteen-year-old singer-songwriter Laura Nyro gained enough buzz from her debut album to play at the Monterey Pop Festival, where, legend has it, she flopped so miserably that she left the stage in tears. However, Columbia Records head Clive Davis liked what he saw, and when she auditioned for him in a darkened rehearsal room, he was blown away by her performance and her brilliant songs.[9] Her first album for the label, *Eli and the Thirteenth Confession* (1968), still sounds remarkable today. The song cycle flows from street-corner soul to jazzy torch songs to theatrical anthems, while also yielding timeless songs in "Eli's Comin'" and "Stoned Soul Picnic." Over it all was her voice, a powerful instrument that ranged from full-throated wails to the smoky phrasing of a cabaret chanteuse.

Nyro followed up this breakthrough with releases that varied in both sonics and tone: the harrowingly dark and spare *New York Tendaberry* (1969); the warm and inviting *Christmas and the Beads of Sweat* (1970); and the soul-song covers album *Gonna Take a Miracle* (1971), the latter a genuinely miraculous collaboration with vocal trio Labelle. Shy and artistically uncompromising, Nyro took a five-year hiatus from music in the middle of the 1970s, permanently stalling her career, but not before directly influencing bigger stars that decade, like the young jazz-rock beatnik Rickie Lee Jones, power-pop whiz and balladeer Todd Rundgren, and even magna diva Barbra Streisand.

Nyro's life and music could have run an entirely different course if she had accepted an offer to be the lead singer in a jazz-rock band that had just lost their frontman. Back in the late 1960s, Al Kooper, still best known today as the organ player on Bob Dylan's "Like A Rolling Stone," initially led Blood, Sweat & Tears. Technically, Kooper was actually one of the several cofounders of the group, but he was certainly the spokesman in 1968, when he told *Rolling Stone*'s Jann Wenner how he wanted to create a band focused on horns, citing a royal flush of jazz fusioneer influences: James Brown, The Beatles, Ray

Charles, and even Maynard Ferguson,[10] the jazz bandleader who first introduced Joe Zawinul to Wayne Shorter. The first version of Blood, Sweat & Tears with Kooper was thus an octet, with a four-piece brass section and a rock section including drummer Bobby Colomby, known later for giving Jaco Pastorius his record deal. Their debut album, *Child Is Father to the Man* (1968), is a fascinating hybrid, based strongly in the hippie blues and pastel psychedelia of the time but with sterling horn charts playing over every track. However lovely the music may be, the sound of jazz sometimes takes second place to the sumptuous pop sound of the Moody Blues.

When the time came to record a follow-up, Kooper was out of the band, pushed out by that old bugbear of musical differences. After being approached to replace him, Nyro had to be talked out of joining by her devoted manager, a young David Geffen, who believed in her as a solo artist. Instead, Blood, Sweat & Tears hired a leather-lunged Canadian named David Clayton-Thomas to sing her song "And When I Die" for their self-titled sophomore release, as well as breakthrough hits like "You've Made Me So Very Happy" and "Spinning Wheel." Now a grooving jazzy behemoth, the band swung through a version of Traffic's "Smiling Phases" and swerved into a hot Latin interlude on their cover of Billie Holiday's signature tune, "God Bless the Child." *Blood, Sweat & Tears* would even go on to win Album of the Year at the Grammys, beating out stiff competition like The Beatles' *Abbey Road* and *Johnny Cash at San Quentin*.[11]

Unfortunately, Clayton-Thomas's immigration status eclipsed the band's brief time in the sun. Threatened with the deportation of their lead singer, the band was essentially forced by the Nixon administration to promote America on a 1970 tour of Iron Curtain countries like Yugoslavia, Poland, and Romania. When they returned to the United States, they described their genuine shock at the repression in the Communist bloc and were swiftly labeled as government stooges by the counterculture press.[12] With their street cred permanently ruined, Blood, Sweat & Tears soon faced scathing reviews and declining sales, eventually becoming a legacy act with a revolving door of band members. It remains one of popular music's weirder tragedies, especially since the album *Blood, Sweat & Tears* was a template for so many albums released in the next decade.

That album's producer was James William Guercio, who was simultaneously working with another big band, combining rock energy with bold jazzy brass. Composed of Windy City club-gig veterans, this septet called themselves the Big Thing, and then Chicago Transit Authority, and finally just Chicago. Unlike Blood, Sweat & Tears, which regularly changed band members and relied heavily on outside material, Chicago had a remarkably steady lineup through most of the 1970s and boasted three strong songwriters in keyboardist Robert Lamm, guitarist Terry Kath, and trombonist James Pankow.

Lamm particularly shined on the group's debut, a double album called *The Chicago Transit Authority* (1969), where he wrote such delightfully breezy jazz-rock hits as "Beginnings," "Does Anybody Really Know What Time It Is?," and "Questions 67 and 68." Meanwhile, Kath showcased his mastery of six strings, bending notes in various gritty bluesy solos or sculpting a gnarled seven-minute noisefest called "Free Form Guitar" that could slot in nicely on an early-1980s Sonic Youth record. The other songs are either delightfully messy jams or have glorious horns blasting fanfares every few bars. Chicago continued to mesh jazz horns and rock on their second album, called simply *Chicago* (1970), and their third, called *Chicago III* (1971), and they did so in ways both beautiful and baroque. Chicago's sunny disposition and polished musicianship appealed to millions of record-buying pop fans, but these same traits also repelled hipster tastemakers, who effectively labeled the band as terminally uncool.

As the 1970s progressed, the band gradually lived down to that reputation, as the hits kept getting bigger and blander. At the same time, the jazz influence kept getting smaller, with the exception of *Chicago VII*'s opening twenty-five minutes of sizzling instrumental jazz-funk and sassy brass. Eventually the commercial lure of treacly ballads like "If You Leave Me Now" trumped musical adventurism, and by the end of the decade, Chicago were rewarded on the charts—and derided in the press—as a schmaltz-rock juggernaut.

At the same time, a fusionesque soul-funk juggernaut stormed the pop charts during the 1970s. Earth, Wind & Fire used funk and soul as a base rather than rock, but their founder and leader, Maurice White, had a jazz musical background. White grew up in Chicago and became a session drummer for Chess Records in the mid-1960s, which is where he met pianist Ramsey Lewis, who had just scored a major soul-jazz hit called "The 'In' Crowd" in 1965. Lewis took a shine to White and brought him aboard on drums, and for the next few years, they moved up from small clubs to premiere venues like Carnegie Hall. All the while, White learned how to be a bandleader by watching his mentor.[13]

In 1969, White went out on his own and formed EWF. By the time of their 1971 self-titled debut, the band was a sprawling eleven-person unit with killer grooves and soulful group vocals to rival Sly and the Family Stone. Their early albums clearly reflected jazz fusion's influence, with longer instrumental jams that had the lush feel of a classic CTI Records platter. Once 1974's *Open Our Eyes* came around, EWF had a stable team of regulars: Maurice's brother Verdine on bass, Larry Dunn on keyboards, Al McKay on guitar, Ralph Johnson on drums, Andrew Woolfolk on reeds, and Philip Bailey on vocals with his trademark angelic falsetto. This group pared the songs down to a tighter length, but many were still flush with the piano vamps and Afro-Brazilian rhythms that kept true to the band's jazz roots.

EWF's 1975 album *That's the Way of the World* finally made them superstars, with radio staples like the slow-burning title track, the sultry ballad "Reasons," and the blissfully frenetic funk of "Shining Star," which hit the top spot on Billboard's Hot 100.[14] As White put it in his memoir, the album was such a success that "Columbia Records wanted another album, like, yesterday."[15] Loath to take a break from a lucrative tour, White decided to record a double album, called *Gratitude* (1975), with three sides live and one studio. Even the smoothest songs and the tightest funk workouts have room to breathe here, and the horn players blow sparks and flames like joyously soulful dragons. The best moment on the record comes at the top of side two, with an incandescent version of Ramsey Lewis's "Sun Goddess." White and several of his EWF brethren had recorded the original for Lewis's 1974 album of the same name, and this eight-minute, summery jazz-funk zephyr became an unlikely massive radio hit. This success pleased White to no end, as he could return the favor to the mentor who had brought him up in the first place.[16]

Even as EWF continued to cement its place as one of the greatest funk and soul bands of all time, White always referred to jazz as his roots. In his final years when he was writing his memoir, he continued to look back fondly on the *Gratitude* era as special, one where he could balance creating beloved hits with an expansive, genre-free take on music. "We were stretching out," he wrote. "We were an R&B band. We were a jazz band. We were a pop band. We were a world music band. We were an Afro-Cuban band. We were feeling the power of our musical diversity, and so were our audiences."[17]

*****

"Jazz is not dead, it just smells funny." Ever since 1973, when Frank Zappa drawled this quip, countless cynical fans and writers have quoted it to deliver a nasty take on jazz's fragile future. At the time, Zappa was one of popular music's most quotable rock stars, thanks to his formidable intelligence, rapacious wit, and often repellent arrogance. These days, this particular joke has gone stale from overuse, but what's still funny about it is that Zappa was actually a pioneering rock star who incorporated jazz and became a master jazz guitarist. By the time he threw out this offhand line, he had focused on making excellent jazz fusion records for at least four years.

Perhaps Zappa mocked jazz because he considered himself an avant-garde composer first and foremost. After all, he also regularly insulted rock music as brain-dead and stupid, even when he was enjoying his greatest commercial success by playing it. With his original 1960s band, the Mothers of Invention, Zappa changed how audiences heard popular music by creating musical collages that smashed together hard rock, doo-wop, contemporary classical, musique concrète, and absurdist satire. The Mothers were versatile multi-instrumentalists who could change styles on a dime, even when Zappa was increasingly introducing chunks of jazz fusion into this decidedly lumpy gravy. In 1969, he released *Hot Rats*, a straight-up smooth-and-groovy fusion record that has been an urtext for budding jazz guitarists ever since. And as he entered the 1970s, his musical output split in two, between smutty comedy live albums that have aged poorly and instrumental albums that are still a pleasurable mash-up of electric Miles Davis, Mahavishnu Orchestra, and Chicago's horn section.

By the early 1970s, Zappa toured with a genuinely hot jazz fusion band that could keep up with the vertiginous twists and turns in his compositions. Most important were keyboardist George Duke and Ruth Underwood, the latter an astonishingly fast and precise percussionist on xylophones, marimbas, and vibraphones. By December 1973, when Zappa began recording the live double *Roxy & Elsewhere*, his band also included drummer Chester Thompson, who went on to play with Weather Report and prog legends Genesis; keyboardist Don Preston, a Mothers veteran dating back to the mid-1960s; Napoleon Murphy Brock, a reedman and singer that Zappa had recently seen playing in a Hawaiian nightclub;[18] and the trio of Fowler brothers, consisting of bassist Tom, trombonist Bruce, and trumpeter Walt. All of these musicians could play Zappa music, then loosen it up with funk and swing; the whole album has a loose, almost rubbery feel that throbs with the thrill of taking music to its complex limits while still making it fun. And the famous quote about smelly jazz is right there, six-and-a-half minutes into the final track, "Be-Bop Tango (Of the Old Jazzmen's Church)." Here's where Zappa brings audience members on stage to compete in a jazz-improv dance competition. When you hear him say the line—in contrast to reading it—Zappa doesn't sound nasty at all. In fact, it sounds like he's having a blast.

Over in England, Jeff Beck was also shedding the shackles of rock strictures and feeling free in the fusion faith. He was one of the three iconic guitarists that emerged from the 1960s British group the Yardbirds. The other two, Eric Clapton and Jimmy Page, went on to stellar mainstream careers, but largely stayed based in rock, no matter how rococo Cream or Led Zeppelin could get. A player who pairs a bristling tone with uncanny precision, Beck took his thrilling technique and went somewhere far weirder as the 1970s progressed. When he left the Yardbirds, Beck's solo albums veered from raucous hard rock into generic funk rock, until—as he told the press at the time—he was finding more inspiration in fusion stars like Billy Cobham and Return to Forever bassist Stanley Clarke.[19]

Their influence is felt most strongly on *Blow by Blow* (1975). On this mostly instrumental album produced by The Beatles' George Martin, Beck's guitar sounds utterly sassy in a jazz-funk context that overflows with throbbing bass, layers of polyrhythmic keyboards, and even moments of symphonic excess worthy of Deodato's "Also Sprach Zarathustra." *Blow by Blow* remains a fabulous listening experience, and it became Beck's highest charting album, reaching No. 4 on the Billboard pop chart.[20] *Wired* (1976) was almost as good and almost as successful. Thanks to Mahavishnu Orchestra's synth dynamo Jan Hammer, strutting jazz-funk gives way to stomping prog-rock fusion, and fortunately the good tunes on *Wired* keep the music from sliding into brazen bombast. But by the 1980s and beyond, Beck moved away from this era and chose to apply his pyrotechnic guitar to faceless hard rock. Oddly, Beck disowned his successful jazz fusion years as he got older. In 2010, he told *Guitar Player* how fusion is "a bad word now," how he regretted mixing genres, and how he should have just stayed with "earthy rock and roll." He even said he wished he'd never recorded *Blow by Blow*, what many consider his best solo album: "It just reminds me of flared trousers and double-breasted jackets."[21]

Carlos Santana would certainly never regret mixing genres, as it's what he's done since his very start as a musician. Born in a rural Mexican town and raised in Tijuana, his father was a mariachi bandleader who passed down a pride in his country's traditional music, even as he was drawn to rock 'n' roll like any eager teenager in the late 1950s. By the start of the 1960s, teenage Carlos was playing guitar on three-chord songs in gritty Tijuana strip clubs,[22] and by the end of the decade, he and his self-titled band were stealing the show at Woodstock with an incendiary set that welded together Latin music and acid rock. Santana scored radio hits with "Black Magic Woman" and "Oye Como Va" and went platinum on their first three records, including *Abraxas* (1970), which has been a dorm-room staple for generations of college students. Multiracial, multicultural, and multigenre, here was a band that had spiraled into stardom by not recognizing boundaries.

And then in 1972, Santana released *Caravanserai*, which launched a whole new phase in the band's evolution: largely instrumental, with extended tracks combining elements of Afro-Cuban music, Brazilian samba, and incandescent jazz-rock into a swirling maelstrom of piercingly loud bliss. A beautiful record, it was also far from the commercial sound they'd been enjoying. This new music was deeply spiritual, and it became even more so during the Caravanserai tour when the Godfather of Fusion, Larry Coryell, introduced him to his new guru, Sri Chinmoy. Before long, Carlos was joining John McLaughlin in the studio to record the loud homage to their master, *Love Devotion Surrender* (1973),[23] while the more rock-oriented members of the band—singer/keyboardist Gregg Rolie and guitarist Neal Schon—left the group to form a little stadium-rock ensemble called Journey.

From thereon out, Carlos and the newly configured Santana emerged, with a particularly key addition in two fusion keyboardists: Tom Coster and Richard Kermode; Santana joked that they were his band's Keith Jarrett and Chick Corea, respectively.[24] Over a bed of shimmering electric keys and boiling drums, Santana expanded further into a widescreen jazz-rock fusion on their next two studio albums, *Welcome* (1973) and *Borboletta* (1974). *Welcome* added the eccentric but soulful vocals of Leon Thomas, best known for singing on Pharoah Sanders's famous free jazz hymn, "The Creator Has a Master Plan," while *Borboletta* was even more explicitly aligned with the jazz fusion of the time—guests included Return to Forever's Airto Moreira, Flora Purim, and Stanley Clarke—and its breezy, humid feel sounds like a road trip from a Bahian beach into the Amazon rainforest. In between these two grand projects, however, emerged a true magnum opus: a Japan-only live triple album, *Lotus* (1974), recorded at Osaka's Koseinenkin Hall on July 3–4, 1973. Carlos and Santana do indeed play many hits off *Abraxas* here—*hola*, "Oye Como Va"—but they're folded into nonstop Afro-Latin jazz fusion that burns for an exhilarating two hours with the intensity of electric Miles Davis and soars with the spiritual ecstasy of the Mahavishnu Orchestra. *Lotus* is arguably one of the greatest jazz fusion documents, period—no matter that it was released by a musician who still identified primarily as a rock star.

Even if it became less fashionable as the decade moved into the next, Carlos Santana never abandoned the idea that all musical ideas can converge happily. When he released his 2014 memoir, *The Universal Tone*, he described this fusion—in the literal sense—as a spiritual practice. "[W]ith it ego disappears and energy takes over. You realize that you are not one alone; you are connected to everyone," he wrote. "Suddenly the music compels people to go against what they thought was aesthetically solid for themselves, and what used to fit so well then feels really uncomfortable. It raises people's consciousness and stops the static so they can hear the forgotten song within."[25]

*****

As the 1970s rolled toward the 1980s, jazz fusion among rock musicians became less de rigueur and more dead on arrival. Punk and disco emerged and delivered a jolt to popular music. The relative simplicity of these new genres was refreshing and produced many life-changing masterworks of their own, but at the time they were also a harsh rebuke to complex music like prog rock and jazz fusion. And with fusion becoming smoother and acoustic jazz raising its traditionalist head, rock artists reasonably turned away.

One band that leaned in instead was Steely Dan. Formed in 1971 by two Bard College classmates, keyboardist/singer Donald Fagen and bassist/guitarist Walter Becker, the band progressed further into jazz fusion through the 1970s. Even as a ten-year-old growing up in New Jersey, jazz was Fagen's first love and a means of mental escape in dull suburbia.[26] As they moved through the 1970s, Steely Dan transitioned from rock songs with earworm choruses, like "Reelin' in the Years" from *Can't Buy a Thrill* (1972), to complex tunes mixing in Latin and jazz-funk, like "Rikki Don't Lose That Number" from *Pretzel Logic* (1974) and "Kid Charlemagne" from *The Royal Scam* (1976).

By the time they recorded *Aja* over many months in 1976 and 1977, Steely Dan was less a band than a recording project, where Fagen and Becker worked with popular music's most accomplished and polished session musicians and then notoriously subjected them to a fastidious search for sonic perfection. The top-shelf talent included funk bassist Chuck Rainey; a pantheon of legendary jazz, soul, and rock drummers like Steve Gadd, Bernard Purdie, and Jim Keltner; Joni Mitchell jazz-rock alums Tom Scott and Larry Carlton; pianist/percussionist Victor Feldman, who played with Ronnie Scott in the UK in the 1950s and with Miles Davis in the United States in the early 1960s; and Wayne Shorter himself wailing away on tenor sax on *Aja*'s title track. Somehow, Fagen and Becker managed to meld all these artistic contributions into a consistently sleek sound that mixed both jazz-rock *and* jazz-funk into catchy pop songs—so catchy that three of them ("Peg," "Josie," and "Deacon

Blues") cracked the top 40 of the Billboard Hot 100 singles chart. *Aja* was the hottest album in the band's history, hitting No. 3 on the Billboard 200,[27] and almost fifty years later, it was still their only album to reach double-platinum status.[28] They couldn't quite repeat the trick on 1980's *Gaucho*, which took three arduous years to make. The duo burned through their budget, employed more than forty musicians, and took perfection to such an obsessive degree they wore the oxide off the tape of one song by listening to it too many times.[29] Fed up with each other, the duo went their separate ways and wouldn't release another Steely Dan album again for twenty years.

1980 was also the year that Van Morrison dropped out of public consciousness, following up an acclaimed album, *Into the Music* (1979), with an uncompromising and mystical jazz fusion album called *Common One*. The irony is that Morrison became revered internationally just a dozen years earlier by releasing an uncompromising and mystical jazz fusion album called *Astral Weeks*. Back in 1968, Morrison was best known as the lead singer for the raw Northern Irish rock band Them, of "Gloria" fame, and for one sweetly romantic solo hit called "Brown Eyed Girl." But Morrison always had musical tastes far more eclectic than rock and pop. Growing up in Belfast in the 1940s and 1950s, he was raised on his father's record collection, which included country, blues, big-band jazz, and Charlie Parker's bebop records,[30] and he started playing the saxophone as a teenager. Morrison always retained an abiding love for all these genres, but when he recorded *Astral Weeks*, jazz and his native Irish folk music won out.

While recording in New York, Morrison wove long, glorious progressive songs that soared with Celtic soul and floated on a base of lithe acoustic jazz, played by veterans like guitarist Jay Berliner, bassist Richard Davis, and Modern Jazz Quartet drummer Connie Kay. A sublime record, *Astral Weeks* is routinely cited on all-time-best lists of rock albums, as is its follow-up, *Moondance* (1970), whose title track is a swinging jazz tune with little rock styling at all. Both albums cemented Morrison as a solo artist who fused genres into a new thing he dubbed "Caledonia soul music," yielding more radio staples and critical acclaim. He would have a few commercial slumps in the mid-1970s, when his albums took a resolutely mystical turn, but then he bounced back quickly by the end of the decade with the LA-style rock of *Wavelength* (1978) and the horn-driven folky soul of *Into the Music*.

By 1980, however, Morrison was at an artistic crossroads. He wanted to let the songs stretch out beyond the four- or five-minute mark without shaping them into digestible singles and album cuts, and he wanted to explore the "far-out" stuff that had been gestating in his mind for months and years.[31] So he and his septet decamped to the exquisitely named Super Bear Studios in France's Alpes Maritimes, a former Knights Templar monastery that appeared to be haunted[32]—perfect for an album of obscure meditations on gnostic history, literature, and the mystic unknown with titles such as "Haunts of Ancient Peace." With six songs totaling just under an hour, *Common One* certainly stretched out with some far-out stuff but was brought down to earth by the jazz horns of Pee Wee Ellis and Mark Isham.

Needless to say, the album tanked, and critics were completely divided. *Creem*'s Mitchell Cohen called the album a failed attempt to "recapture the epic grandeur of *Astral*

Weeks,"[33] but Lester Bangs argued in the *Village Voice* that it was rapturous and vast "holy music" too easily dismissed by small-minded rock critics.[34] To this listener, at least, *Common One* sounds like a superior jazz fusion record to close out the decade, one that combines the eerie luminosity of Miles Davis's "He Loved Him Madly" with the quiet mystery of a prime ECM release—a beautiful sound, indeed.

Unfortunately, Morrison wouldn't have another radio hit until 1989. This time around, the song was a simple love song called "Have I Told You Lately," whose soft-focus orchestration made it palatable for easy listening stations and weddings 'til kingdom come. By that point, the 1980s were almost over, bright pop and hair metal reigned supreme, and the 1970s jazz fusion era seemed almost forgotten. But that's another story entirely.

Ten Essential 1970s Jazz Fusion Albums by Ten Jazzbo Rockstars

Eli and the Thirteenth Confession, by Laura Nyro (1968)
Blood Sweat and Tears, by Blood Sweat and Tears (1968)
The Chicago Transit Authority, by Chicago (1969)
Roxy & Elsewhere, by Zappa/Mothers (1974)
Lotus, by Santana (1974)
Gratitude, by Earth, Wind & Fire (1975)
Blow by Blow, by Jeff Beck (1975)
Aja, by Steely Dan (1977)
Don Juan's Reckless Daughter, by Joni Mitchell (1977)
Common One, by Van Morrison (1980)

Coda
Jazz Fusion Has Always Been Current, a Joyous Celebration to the Present Day

Of course, jazz fusion didn't just vanish in a plume of cosmic dust once the 1970s passed into the annals of history. Even as neo-traditionalists like Wynton Marsalis began to absorb most of the attention of the press and the adulation of critics, jazz musicians continued to produce albums based on electricity, riffs, and grooves that reached receptive audiences. However, distinct changes in sound and presentation proved the music was entering a new era. First were overall trends in record production, from earthier, analog recordings to shinier albums that relied more on compression and digital technology. The other change was economic: The 1980s also marked the beginning of the long, painful process of consolidation in the record industry, where major labels merged with each other while swallowing smaller labels or merely pushing them into obscurity. Commercial concerns were always important—business is the harsh reality of music, after all—and the vibrant experimentation and cosmic discovery of jazz fusion in the 1970s could no longer be indulged to anything resembling the same degree. Even more, at least in the realm of mainstream jazz fusion, much of the shock of the new had passed by the 1980s, as the music increasingly focused more on technical ability on the one hand and anodyne accessibility on the other.

The crossover music of George Benson and Grover Washington Jr. soon transformed into the dreaded "smooth jazz," a term coined by a market research firm in the 1980s, and which eventually boasted the multiplatinum-selling, ringlet-maned saxman Kenny G as its poster child—or scapegoat, depending on your point of view. "As a result," jazz historian Ted Gioia writes, "jazz would be forever linked with a style of easy listening music that many opinion leaders in the art form would prefer not to exist—or at least not inside the gated jazz community—and which, they griped, simply encroached on the livelihood of legit acts in their field."[1] But while this music has never been pure, the reality was not as simple as the perception. Smooth jazz produced a wealth of vapid music, but it also worked in tandem with the mellow and jazzy "quiet storm" radio format that welcomed legends like Benson, nurtured beautiful soul singers like Luther Vandross and Anita Baker, and helped popularize the band Sade, whose luscious and sultry hits "Smooth Operator" and "The Sweetest Taboo" also stormed the pop charts.

In 1985, Pat Metheny collaborated with David Bowie on "This Is Not America," the single from *The Falcon and the Snowman* movie soundtrack, and a year later he started releasing records on David Geffen's major label. Metheny continued to make best-selling music that was easy on the ears, but he did so by blending his lyrical guitar with electronics and Brazilian music into breathlessly cinematic symphonies. In between, he also released a collaboration, called *Song X* (1986), with free jazz pioneer Ornette Coleman, thus proving that even the most successful jazz fusioneers could still swerve for a stylistic adventure. Another artist who carried the fusion torch was singer/bassist Sting, who broke away from the stadium band the Police in the mid-1980s. A trio of virtuoso musicians, the Police always had a jazz sensibility lurking behind their blend of new wave, reggae, and rock, but Sting brought it forward. He formed a new band composed of young jazz musicians, including pianist Kenny Kirkland, Weather Report drummer Omar Hakim, and even Wynton Marsalis's older brother Branford on sax. Together, they released two smash jazz-tinged pop records in *The Dream of the Blue Turtles* (1985) and . . . *Nothing Like the Sun* (1987), and one uproarious, pop-tinged jazz record, the live double album *Bring on the Night* (1986).

Underneath the mainstream lurked a whole school of adventure, especially in New York, where it came with a bit more urban attitude than cosmic consciousness. As early as the late 1970s, jazz merged with punk in a genre called No Wave, with bands like DNA and James Chance & the Contortions blasting eardrums with loud skronk and fearless improvisation. Come the 1980s, the downtown jazz-funk scene boasted gritty groups like Material and Defunkt, as well as avant-garde auteurs like guitarist James Blood Ulmer and bassist Jamaaladeen Tacuma. Both Ulmer and Tacuma originally gained renown playing for that same free jazz pioneer, Ornette Coleman, who had himself formed his own off-kilter jazz-funk group called Prime Time. By 1988, Coleman and the band were on a major label with the album *Virgin Beauty*, which featured none other than Grateful Dead guitarist Jerry Garcia as a special guest. Meanwhile, two more crucial guitarists emerged from this scene. First, Bill Frisell gained fame by creating serene beauty, haunting soundscapes, wistful Americana, and the violent sound of twisted wreckage with six strings and an array of pedal effects. He initially made his name on a series of albums for ECM, but he too followed in Metheny's footsteps, joining a major label and becoming a major recording star to the present day. Then there is Vernon Reid, who began his career in the early 1980s with experimental jazz-rock drummer Ronald Shannon Jackson's group, The Decoding Society, and then formed Living Colour, a blistering hard-rock band that has earned many radio hits while folding in R&B, funk, and avant-garde jazz technique.

Then hip-hop brought the spirit and sound of 1970s jazz fusion back into the consciousness of a new generation, thanks to the profusion of used jazz, soul, and jazz fusion vinyl records in record stores throughout America's cities. Hip-hop producers and artists went crate-digging and found countless albums laden with the pure gold of drum breaks, bass ostinatos, horn blasts, and shimmering Fender Rhodes electric piano—all of which could be sampled and cut-up and turned into tracks that an MC could rap over. Top artists like Eric B. & Rakim, DJ Jazzy Jeff & the Fresh Prince, Stetsasonic, Gang Starr, and the Beastie Boys were among the early acts to spin these tracks into a new generation of crossover hits.

With the 1990s, hip-hop's love affair with jazz was official. Bands like Digable Planets and A Tribe Called Quest based their entire sound on the smokiest sides of jazz fusion—the latter even enlisted the legendary bassist Ron Carter as a guest on their smash sophomore album, *The Low End Theory* (1991). They were joined in this vibe by artists across the United States, from

Pete Rock & C.L. Smooth in New York to Common in Chicago to the Pharcyde in LA. A new concept came out of Philadelphia with the Roots, a large ensemble led by drummer Questlove and its MC, Black Thought, who played tough yet elastic jazz-hip-hop with live instruments. Then in 1993, Gang Starr's MC, Guru, made the linkage of genres explicit with his solo album *Jazzmatazz, Volume 1*. Subtitled "An Experimental Fusion of Hip-hop and Jazz," the record welcomed guest spots by 1970s legends like keyboardist Lonnie Liston Smith, vibraphonist Roy Ayers, and none other than the professor himself, Donald Byrd. The same year, US3 even reached No. 9 on the Billboard Hot 100 with "Cantaloop (Flip Fantasia), bringing the jazz-hip-hop connection mainstream."[2] Built around a sample of Herbie Hancock's "Cantaloupe Island," it was the standout track from *Hand on the Torch* (1993), wherein Blue Note let the UK group have free rein sampling its bank of legendary recordings.

Hip-hop may have led the way, but other genres emerged in the 1990s, each of which reached back to the 1970s. The word "neo-soul" also had corporate-marketing origins, but it has been used ever since to describe singers like D'Angelo, Jill Scott, Maxwell, and Erykah Badu, all of whom were taking the funk, the jazz, *and* the hip-hop beats into new realms of expression. In the UK, drum 'n' bass took off, as electronic DJs like Goldie, Grooverider, and LTJ Bukem matched the starkest, darkest elements of jazz fusion to frantic polyrhythms reaching 180 beats per minute. Clubs in Europe also welcomed acid jazz. Despite the freaky name, the music was really just tight jazz fusion that would have fit in nicely on the CTI record label. A bigger trend that swept through club culture around the world was "lounge" music, where original artists created original mellow jazz electronica for chill-out rooms or where DJs like Gilles Peterson created whole radio shows from the cream of obscure classics in desperate need of rediscovery.

With the new millennium, jazz fusion now has musicians merging all these genres in new and exciting ways. One of its most exciting epicenters is Los Angeles. First, there are electronic artists like Flying Lotus and Georgia Anne Muldrow, who create dense, glitchy albums out of the elements of jazz fusion—rumbling bass, complex rhythms, and live instruments—and then chop and arrange the music to exhilarating, disorienting effect. Rapper Kendrick Lamar enlisted Flying Lotus to work on his landmark double album *To Pimp a Butterfly* (2015), which is so rich with the heritage of Black music (and so deep with its lyrical themes of Black identity and struggle) that Lamar rose to the highest level of American artists in any medium. Two years later, he would win the Pulitzer Prize for Music with his full-length follow-up, *DAMN*. Lamar also turned to the expertise of the West Coast Get Down, a collective of school friends who grew up together in LA, who are openly devoted to reviving jazz fusion, and who are proud to be called "the Wu-Tang Clan of jazz."[3]

The two most famous members of this multitalented crew are bassist/singer Thundercat and saxophonist Kamasi Washington. Thundercat has an incredible resume: He launched his career by playing with rapper Snoop Dogg and then thrash-punk band Suicidal Tendencies—replacing Robert Trujillo, who left to join Metallica[4]—and has since collaborated with artists as wide-ranging as the three-sister rock band Haim, electronic psychedelic savant Tame Impala, and even the fictional cartoon quartet Gorillaz. His own albums, like

Drunk (2017) and *It Is What It Is* (2020), sound like 1970s jazz fusion pushed through a millennial Cuisinart with their mix of electronic mayhem, seismic bass, and his dreamlike, soulful vocals. Washington, meanwhile, is the master of the magnum opus. Assembling a musical cast of dozens that includes an electroacoustic jazz band, an orchestra, and a chorale of voices, he crafts three-hour albums like *The Epic* (2015) and *Heaven and Earth* (2018) that burst open like an endless landscape of lotus flowers. Here you can feel the mysterious wonder of Miles Davis, the spiritual grooves of the Mwandishi band, the musical pleasure of a grandiose CTI release, and the proud, uncompromising artistry of an ECM genius.

Worldwide, many of jazz fusion's contemporary advances are coming from women, a welcome change in a historically male-dominated genre. Like many prodigies in this book, Terri Lyne Carrington started young, playing percussion as a kid with jazz greats like Rahsaan Roland Kirk and Oscar Peterson.[5] But as a female jazz drummer, she was considered a rarity when she launched her own solo career in the 1980s. Thankfully, she's become an inspirational elder for musicians in the decades since: In 2007 she became a professor at Boston's Berklee College of Music, and in 2018 she founded the school's Institute of Jazz and Gender Justice to break down patriarchal biases and promote the role of women in jazz. She had already made waves doing this in her recording career with her Grammy-winning *The Mosaic Project* (2011), an exceptional album featuring women jazz musicians from various generations and countries, including Patrice Rushen, singers like Dianne Reeves and Labelle's Nona Hendryx, bassist Esperanza Spalding, clarinetist Anat Cohen, and drummer

Sheila E. By 2019, she released a sprawling double album, called *Waiting Game*, that incorporated electronics, turntables, funk, collective improvisation, and a wealth of fresh young musicians into a moving meditation on Black Lives Matter and other social traumas afflicting the United States.

Carrington's not alone in making some of the most exciting and most lauded music in jazz and jazz fusion. Esperanza Spalding has her own Grammy-winning career, with albums that meld jazz with soul and Brazilian music, such as the luminous *Milton + Esperanza* (2024) her collaboration with legendary singer Milton Nascimento. In New York, saxophonist Lakecia Benjamin came up as a backing musician to rapper Missy Elliott and singer Alicia Keys,[6] and now fronts her own band that spotlights funk and R&B horn arrangements worthy of James Brown or any Stax Records classic. Carrington even produced Benjamin's fourth album, the Grammy-nominated *Phoenix* (2023). Over in London, saxophonist Nubya Garcia fuses jazz with modern electronics and music from her Caribbean heritage, like reggae, calypso, and Colombian cumbia. Her breakthrough album, *Source* (2020), even had an accompanying album of electronic remixes. Jazz fusion's greatest strength is the way it welcomes new voices and sounds, and so it is in very good hands with this next generation.

What makes this circumstance even happier is how this next generation has such a direct line to the old. While Terri Lyne Carrington is producing albums and promoting the careers of the brightest young women in jazz, she is also a bridge to an earlier time, having played with the likes of 1970s jazz fusion greats such as Wayne Shorter, Herbie Hancock, and George

Duke. Flying Lotus, aka Steven Ellison, is the grandnephew of Alice Coltrane, John Coltrane's widow, and one of spiritual jazz's guiding lights in the 1960s and 1970s. And as Patrice Rushen likes to point out, she went to Locke High School back in the day with the musician dads of Thundercat and Kamasi Washington; she remembers when each of them was born.[7] It's a lovely, literal metaphor for how the spirit of 1970s jazz fusion lives on today, even as its original pioneers get older and increasingly leave us behind on this Spaceship Earth.

It's also a sign of the genre's continuity. No matter how time-locked some of the music may sound today, and no matter how often closed-minded cynics may want to lock it all away permanently, so many of the world's best artists continue to connect with audiences through jazz fusion. And they do so with its spiritual inspiration, tuneful appeal, booty-shaking joy, or all three at once. Because of its enduring qualities for connection, jazz fusion has been remarkably resilient—and because of its ability to welcome wide currents of music, jazz fusion promises to be as current as it's ever been.

10 Essential Tracks of 1970s Jazz Fusion

"Pharaoh's Dance," by Miles Davis (*Bitches Brew*, 1970)
"Birdland," by Weather Report (*Heavy Weather*, 1977)
"Chameleon," by Herbie Hancock (*Head Hunters*, 1973)
"Birds of Fire," by Mahavishnu Orchestra (*Birds of Fire*, 1973)
"Spain," by Chick Corea & Return to Forever (*Light as a Feather*, 1973)
"Black Byrd," by Donald Byrd (*Black Byrd*, 1973)
"Harlem River Drive," by Bobbi Humphrey (*Blacks and Blues*, 1973)
"Also Sprach Zarathustra (2001)," by Deodato (*Prelude*, 1973)
"Across the Heartland," by Pat Metheny Group (*American Garage*, 1979)
"Overture—Cotton Avenue," by Joni Mitchell (*Don Juan's Reckless Daughter*, 1977)

Notes

Prelude

1. Hunt, pp. 87–88, 90. Quoted in Bianchi, p. 285.
2. Taylor, pp. 21–25.
3. https://wyntonmarsalis.org/news/entry/saint-or-sinner-when-wynton-marsalis-comes-marching-in
4. Taylor, pp. 21–25.
5. https://mixmag.net/feature/patrice-rushen-interview-jazz-rnb-singer-sampling
6. Palmer, p. 22.

Chapter 1

1. Gleason, *Bitches Brew*.
2. Szwed, p. 9.
3. Szwed, p. 15.
4. Hancock, pp. 103–104.
5. Goaty, Seidel, and Bergerot. p. 180.
6. Davis, Miles, pp. 291–293.
7. Tingen, p. 58.
8. Davis, Miles, p. 297.
9. Davis, Miles, p. 310.

10 Watrous, p. 1.

11 https://www.riaa.com/gold-platinum/?tab_active=default-award&se=miles%20davis&col=label&ord=desc

12 Davis, Miles, p. 311.

13 Davis, Miles, p. 311.

14 Goaty, Seidel, and Bergerot, p. 194.

15 Cook and Morton, p. 411.

16 Szwed, pp. 324–325.

17 Szwed, p. 326.

18 Tingen, p. 137.

19 http://music.hyperreal.org/artists/brian_eno/onland-txt.html

20 https://www.whosampled.com/sample/376141/The-Orb-Slug-Dub-Miles-Davis-Calypso-Frelimo/

21 Tingen, p. 164.

22 Szwed, p. 324.

23 Davis, Miles, p. 336.

24 Davis, Miles, p. 339.

25 Szwed, p. 399.

26 Gottlieb, ed. p. 909.

27 Watrous, p. 1.

28 Giddins, p. 354.

Chapter 2

1 https://www.weatherreportdiscography.org/mr-gone/

2 Bianchi, p. 241.

3 https://www.riaa.com/gold-platinum/?tab_active=default-award&se=weather+report#search_section

4 https://www.billboard.com/charts/billboard-200/1977-08-27/

5 Davis, Miles, p. 294.

6 Bianchi, pp. 82–83.

7 https://forbassplayersonly.com/interview-alphonso-johnson-2/

8 Mercer, pp. 143–144.

9 Bianchi, p. 159.

10 Mercer, p. 145.

11 https://www.npr.org/2013/02/02/170882668/wayne-shorter-on-jazz-how-do-you-rehearse-the-unknown

12 Bianchi, p. 89.

13 https://www.robertchristgau.com/get_artist.php?name=Weather+Report

14 https://davidaldridge.wordpress.com/2022/03/29/joe-zawinul-the-somewhat-long-lost-interview-about-drummers-and-weather-report/

15 https://www.cookrichmondfuneralhome.com/obituary/herschel-dwellingham

16 https://www.whosampled.com/album/Weather-Report/Sweetnighter/

17 Mercer, p. 161.

18 https://www.weatherreportdiscography.org/mysterious-traveller/

19 Bianchi, pp. 187–191.

20 Bianchi, pp. 215–219.

21 Bianchi, p. 225.

22 Bianchi, pp. 222–223.

23 Bianchi, p. 226.

24 Berendt, p. 644.

25 Walls, "Weather Report."

26 Bianchi, p. 252.

27 Mercer, p. 185.

28 Sutcliffe, "Weather Report."

29 Bianchi, pp. 326–327.

30 Bianchi, p. 324.

31 Bianchi, p. 330.

32 https://jacopastorius.com/life/

33 Bianchi, pp. 408–411.

34 Rensin, "Weather Report."

Chapter 3

1 *Sunlight*, by Herbie Hancock, album cover credits. Columbia, 1978.

2 Hancock, p. 210.

3 https://www.officialcharts.com/songs/herbie-hancock-i-thought-it-was-you/

4 Hancock, p. 214.

5 Hancock, p. 3.

6 Hancock, p. 5–6.

7 Hancock, p. 4–5.

8	Hancock, p. 21.
9	Hancock, p. 23.
10	Hancock, p. 25–29.
11	*Zawinul*, by Joe Zawinul, album cover credits, 1970.
12	https://www.huffpost.com/entry/tribute-to-miles-a-conver_b_883658
13	Hancock, p. 42–43.
14	Hancock, p. 46.
15	Davis, Miles, p. 263.
16	Hancock, p. 116.
17	Gluck, p. 59.
18	"Best Seller", p. 32.
19	Gluck, p. 25.
20	Gluck, p. 86.
21	Coryell and Friedman, p. 162.
22	Hancock, p. 143.
23	Hancock, p. 153.
24	https://www.herbiehancock.com/music/discography/album/671/
25	Hancock, p. 169–170.
26	Pond, p. 111–112.
27	Pond, p. 29.
28	https://www.herbiehancock.com/music/discography/album/673/
29	Pond, p. 80.
30	Andrews, "Herbie Hancock."
31	Hancock, p. 199–201.

32 Giddins, p. 621.

33 Coryell and Friedman, p. 163.

Chapter 4

1 Coryell and Friedman, pp. 87–88.

2 https://richardvacca.com/dec-17-1962-world-meet-tony-williams/

3 Davis, Miles, p. 262.

4 https://richardvacca.com/dec-17-1962-world-meet-tony-williams/

5 Shipton, p. 611.

6 Fellezs, p. 102.

7 Snowden, "Jazz Drummer Tony Williams."

8 Fellezs, p. 95.

9 Nicholson, p. 143.

10 De Barros, "Tony Williams."

11 De Barros, "Tony Williams."

12 https://www.johnmclaughlin.com/musical-life/

13 Harper, pp. 326–327.

14 Berg, p. 16.

15 Harper, pp. 20–23.

16 Harper, pp. 33–34.

17 Harper, p. 62.

18 Nicholson, p. 135.

19 https://www.srichinmoy.org/sri_chinmoy/biography

20 Bernstein, "Larry Coryell."

21 Nicholson, p. 137.

22 Harper, pp. 360–361.

23 Nicholson, pp. 145–146.

24 https://www.billboard.com/charts/billboard-200/1973-04-28/

25 https://www.riaa.com/gold-platinum/?tab_active=default-award&se=birds+of+fire#search_section

26 Cromelin, "The Mahavishnu Orchestra."

27 Alterman, "Rick Laird."

28 Welch, "Mahavishnu Orchestra."

29 Harper, p. 459.

30 https://www.johnmclaughlin.com/2018/01/happy-new-year/

31 https://www.herbiehancock.com/2014/10/19/herbie-hancock-and-chick-corea-announce-spring-2015-tour/

32 https://www.jazzwise.com/features/article/chick-corea-interview-music-can-bring-us-together

33 https://chickcorea.com/bio/1941-71/

34 https://www.wdchof.org/jazz-pianist-chick-corea-was-inducted-into-world-drum-corps-hall-of-fame-in-recognition-of-his-many-distinguished-achievements/

35 https://chelsearecord.com/2021/02/18/appreciation-chick-corea-left-his-heart-in-chelsea/

36 Russonello, p. 21.

37 https://nationaljazzarchive.org.uk/explore/interviews/1621497-chick-corea-interview-1?

38 https://www.robertchristgau.com/get_artist.php?id=3565&name=Return+to+Forever+Featuring+Chick+Corea

39 https://www.grammy.com/artists/chick-corea-and-return-forever/14675

Chapter 5

1 https://www.cbr.com/king-of-the-hill-chuck-mangione/

2 https://southpark.fandom.com/wiki/Where_My_Country_Gone%3F/Trivia

3 https://www.smithsonianmag.com/smithsonian-institution/thats-some-bad-hat-chuck-as-in-mangione-44822892/

4 https://www.chuckmangione.com/bio.html

5 West, "Mangione."

6 https://www.scottyanow.com/FREDDIEHUBBARD.html

7 Stewart, "The Two Audiences of Freddie Hubbard."

8 https://downbeat.com/news/detail/trumpeter-donald-byrd-dies-at-801

9 Havers, p. 324.

10 Havers, p. 319.

11 https://www.bluenote.com/artist/the-mizell-brothers/

12 Yardley, p. 28.

13 https://www.whosampled.com/Donald-Byrd/

14 https://www.arts.gov/honors/jazz/donald-byrd

15 https://amsterdamnews.com/news/2016/04/26/bobbi-humphrey-still-going-strong/

16 https://web.archive.org/web/20190329140037/http://www.bobbihumphrey.net/bio.html

17 Havers, pp. 346–349.

18 https://www.whosampled.com/Bobbi-Humphrey/

19 https://amsterdamnews.com/news/2016/04/26/bobbi-humphrey-still-going-strong/

20 Coryell and Friedman, pp. 67–68.

21 https://billycobham.com/biography

22 Hobart, "Interview."

23 https://www.whosampled.com/sample/20/Massive-Attack-Safe-From-Harm-Billy-Cobham-Stratus/

24 https://dlmediamusic.com/festivals/panama-jazz-festival/panama-jazz-festival-2024/

25 https://www.georgedukemusic.com/the-billy-cobham-george-duke-band-live-on-tour-in-europe

26 https://www.georgedukemusic.com/bio

27 https://www.billboard.com/artist/george-duke/chart-history/tlp/

28 https://www.billboard.com/artist/george-duke/chart-history/blp/

29 http://www.justsoul.altervista.org/interviews/interview63.htm

30 https://kentuckymusichalloffame.com/les-mccann/

31 https://www.jazzwax.com/2024/01/les-mccann-1935-2023.html

32 McCann, Dorn, and Litfin, *Layers*.

33 McCann, Dorn, and Litfin, *Layers*.

34 Swenson, "Les McCann."

35 https://concord.com/artist/patrice-rushen/

36 https://patricerushen.com/career-life

37 Abbey, "Patrice Rushen."

38 https://patricerushen.com/full-length-bio

39 https://mixmag.net/feature/patrice-rushen-interview-jazz-rnb-singer-sampling

40 https://www.georgebenson.com/#about

41 https://youtu.be/A7Oxk6ZRr_M?si=qvcFyn7V5gtwY7S4

42 https://www.riaa.com/gold-platinum/?tab_active=default-award&se=george+benson#search_section

43 https://www.billboard.com/artist/george-benson/chart-history/tlp/

44 Berendt, p. 423.

45 Katz, "George Benson."

46 https://www.billboard.com/artist/george-benson/chart-history/tlp/

47 https://www.billboard.com/artist/bill-withers/

48 https://www.bluenote.com/artist/grover-washington-jr/

49 Kelley, p. 67.

50 https://www.allaboutjazz.com/news/grover-washington-inner-city-blues/

51 https://www.tiktok.com/music/Just-the-Two-of-Us-227302284517642240?lang=en

52 https://www.deseret.com/1995/9/30/19195762/grover-washington-jr-is-smooth-not-shallow/

Chapter 6

1 Havers, pp. 311–319.

2 Davis, Clive, p. 142.

3 https://www.jazzwax.com/2008/05/interview-creed.html
4 https://indianapublicmedia.org/afterglow/creed-taylor-and-the-singers.php
5 Kahn, p. 29.
6 Myers, "The Man Behind All That Jazz."
7 https://www.grammy.com/artists/stan-getz/9156
8 Turner and Kahn, p. 9.
9 Turner and Kahn, p. 143.
10 https://www.billboard.com/artist/deodato/
11 Cook and Morton, p. 130.
12 Nicholson, p. 210.
13 Gioia, p. 437.
14 https://www.ctproduced.com/cti-enters-chapter-xi-bankruptcy/
15 Lake and Griffiths, eds., p. 1.
16 Enwezor and Müller, eds., pp. 31–33.
17 Weber, pp. 98–99.
18 Eicher, Müller, Rehm, and Wojirsch, eds., pp. 9–10.
19 https://ecmrecords.com/artists/keith-jarrett/
20 Gilmore, "Keith Jarrett's Keys to the Cosmos."
21 Lake and Griffiths, eds., p. 246.
22 Lake and Griffiths, eds., p. 343.
23 Williams, "Manfred Eicher."
24 Coryell and Friedman, p. 95.
25 Weber, p. 98.
26 Carr, pp. 58–60.

Chapter 7

1. Yaffe, pp. 220–222.
2. O'Hagan, "Idol Talk."
3. Yaffe, p. 30.
4. Yaffe, pp. 38–39.
5. Yaffe, pp. 256–258.
6. https://www.rollingstone.com/music/music-album-reviews/don-juans-reckless-daughter-199872/
7. https://www.riaa.com/gold-platinum/?tab_active=default-award&se=joni+mitchell&col=certification_date&ord=asc#search_section
8. https://blogs.loc.gov/loc/2023/03/joni-mitchells-conversation-in-the-library/
9. Davis, Clive, pp. 79–80.
10. Wenner, "Blood, Sweat & Tears."
11. https://www.grammy.com/awards/12th-annual-grammy-awards
12. https://www.rollingstone.com/music/music-features/blood-sweat-tears-iron-curtain-tour-movie-1234700472/
13. White, pp. 60–65.
14. https://www.billboard.com/artist/earth-wind-fire/
15. White, p. 191.
16. White, pp. 161–162.
17. White, p. 192.
18. Slaven, p. 199.
19. https://www.guitarplayer.com/players/jeff-beck-blow-by-blow

- **20** https://www.billboard.com/pro/jeff-beck-billboard-chart-history/
- **21** https://www.guitarplayer.com/players/i-shouldnt-have-done-blow-by-blow-jeff-beck-reveals-his-regrets-in-this-hilarious-interview
- **22** Santana, pp. 79–80.
- **23** Santana, pp. 317–321.
- **24** Santana, p. 316.
- **25** Santana, p. 9.
- **26** Sweet, locs. 129 and 4106 of 6569, Kindle.
- **27** https://www.billboard.com/pro/steely-dan-walter-becker-donald-fagen-billboard-chart-hot-100-hits/
- **28** https://www.riaa.com/gold-platinum/?tab_active=default-award&se=steely+dan#search_section
- **29** Sweet, loc. 2533 or 6569, Kindle.
- **30** Heylin, pp. 17–21.
- **31** Heylin, pp. 357–358.
- **32** Heylin, p. 360.
- **33** Cohen, "Van Morrison."
- **34** Heylin, p. 364.

Coda

- **1** Gioia, p. 438.
- **2** https://web.archive.org/web/20170528063226/http://www.billboard.com/artist/430705/us3/chart
- **3** https://milesmosley.com/west-coast-get-down

4 https://www.npr.org/sections/therecord/2013/07/20/203347014/thundercat-on-making-music-outside-the-lines#:~:text=It%20was%20as%20he%20was,shirts,%20got%20his%20stage%20name

5 https://www.bostonmagazine.com/2011/11/29/arts-beat-a-beat-of-her-own/

6 https://lakeciabenjamin.com/about/

7 https://mixmag.net/feature/patrice-rushen-interview-jazz-rnb-singer-sampling

Select Bibliography

Author's note: Listening again and again to hundreds of brilliant albums was the highlight of researching this book, and so was the time spent researching it with the help of dozens of brilliant books, newspaper clips, websites, and magazine articles. Readers here are thus encouraged to further explore the history of jazz and 1970s jazz fusion by diving into these sources below, written by scholars far more advanced than this author. The first references for all other sources can be found in the footnotes.

Abbey, John. "Patrice Rushen: Rushen Invasion!" *Blues & Soul*, March 11, 1980. Retrieved from http://www.rocksbackpages.com/Library/Article/patrice-rushen-rushen-invasion

Alterman, Loraine. "Rick Laird: Why Mahavishnu is Breaking Up." *Rolling Stone*, February 28, 1974. Retrieved from http://www.rocksbackpages.com/Library/Article/rick-laird-why-mahavishnu-is-breaking-up

Andrews, Colman. "Herbie Hancock Sells In." *Phonograph Record*, November 1974. Retrieved from http://www.rocksbackpages.com/Library/Article/herbie-hancock-sells-in

Bianchi, Curt. *Elegant People: A History of the Band Weather Report*. Guilford, Conn.: Backbeat Books, 2021.

"Best Seller: Herbie Hancock—*Fat Albert Rotunda* Wins him a Big Pop Following." *DownBeat*, December 24, 1970, 32.

Bernstein, Adam. "Larry Coryell, Dazzling Guitarist Who Brought Rock Energy to Jazz, Dies at 73." *The Washington Post*, February 21, 2017.

"Best Seller: Herbie Hancock—*Fat Albert Rotunda* Wins him a Big Pop Following." *DownBeat*, December 24, 1970, 32.

Carr, Ian. *Keith Jarrett: The Man and His Music*. London: Grafton Books, 1991.

Cohen, Mitchell. "Van Morrison: Common One." *Creem*, December 1980. Retrieved from http://www.rocksbackpages.com/Library/Article/van-morrison-icommon-onei

Cook, Richard. *It's About That Time: Miles Davis On and Off Record*. New York: Oxford University Press, 2007.

Cook, Richard and Brian Morton. *The Penguin Guide to Jazz on CD*, 7th ed. New York: Penguin Books, 2004.

Coryell, Julie and Laura Friedman. *Jazz-Rock Fusion: The People, The Music*. New York: Dell Publishing, 1978.

Coryell, Larry. *Improvising: My Life in Music*. New York: Backbeat Books, 2007.

Cromelin, Richard. "The Mahavishnu Orchestra, the Section: Civic Auditorium, Santa Monica CA." *Los Angeles Times*, November 13, 1972. Retrieved from http://www.rocksbackpages.com/Library/Article/the-mahavishnu-orchestra-the-section-civic-auditorium-santa-monica-ca

Davis, Clive, with Anthony DeCurtis. *The Soundtrack of My Life*. New York: Simon & Schuster, 2013.

Davis, Miles, with Quincy Troupe. *Miles: The Autobiography*. New York: Simon & Schuster, 1989.

De Barros, Paul. "Tony Williams' Two Decades of Drum Innovation." *DownBeat*, November 1983.

Eicher, Manfred, Lars Müller, Dieter Rehm, and Barbara Wojirsch, eds. *ECM: Sleeves of Desire*. Baden, Switzerland: Lars Müller Publishers, 1996.

Enwezor, Okwui and Markus Müller, eds. *ECM: A Cultural Archaeology*. Munich: Prestel, 2012.

Fellezs, Kevin. *Birds of Fire: Jazz, Rock, Funk, and the Creation of Fusion.* Durham, N.C.: Duke University Press, 2011.

Giddins, Gary. *Visions of Jazz: The First Century.* New York: Oxford University Press, 1998.

Gilmore, Mikal. "Keith Jarrett's Keys to the Cosmos." *Rolling Stone*, January 27, 1979.

Gioia, Ted. *The History of Jazz*, 3rd ed. New York: Oxford University Press, 2021.

Gleason, Ralph J. *Bitches Brew*, by Miles Davis, liner notes, 1970.

Gluck, Bob. *You'll Know When You Get There: Herbie Hancock and the Mwandishi Band.* Chicago: The University of Chicago Press, 2012.

Goaty, Frédéric, Richard Seidel, and Franck Bergerot. *Miles Davis: The Complete Columbia Album Collection*, compact-disc box-set book. Sony Music/Legacy, 2009.

Gottlieb, Robert, ed. *Reading Jazz: A Gathering of Autobiography, Reportage, and Criticism from 1919 to Now.* New York: Vintage, 1996.

Grella, George Jr. *Bitches Brew.* New York: Bloomsbury Academic, 2015.

Hancock, Herbie, with Lisa Dickey. *Possibilities.* New York: Viking, 2014.

Harper, Colin. *Bathed in Lightning: John McLaughlin, the 60s and the Emerald Beyond.* London: Jawbone Press, 2014.

Havers, Richard. *Blue Note: Uncompromising Expression.* London: Thames & Hudson, 2022.

Heylin, Clinton. *Can You Feel the Silence? Van Morrison: A New Biography.* Chicago: Chicago Review Press, 2003.

Hobart, Mike. "Interview: Billy Cobham and His Fusion Jazz Career." *Financial Times*, April 25, 2014.

Hunt, Dennis. "Weather Report's Cloudy Image," *Los Angeles Times*, November 19, 1978, Calendar section, 87–88, 90.

Kahn, Ashley. *The House That Trane Built: The Story Of Impulse Records*. New York: W.W. Norton & Company, 2006.

Katz, Robin. "George Benson: Mr Bad Makes Good." *Sounds*, September 4, 1976. Retrieved from http://www.rocksbackpages.com/Library/Article/george-benson-mr-bad-makes-good

Kelley, Tina. "Grover Washington Jr., 56, Versatile Jazz Musician, Dies." *The New York Times*, December 19, 1999, Section 1, 67.

Lake, Steve and Paul Griffiths. *Horizons Touched: The Music of ECM*. London: Granta, 2007.

McCann, Les, Joel Dorn, and Robert Litfin. *Layers*, by Les McCann, liner notes, 1973.

Mercer, Michelle. *Footprints: The Life and Work of Wayne Shorter*. New York: Jeremy P. Tarcher/Penguin, 2004.

Müller, Lars, ed. *Windfall Light: The Visual Language of ECM*. Baden, Switzerland: Lars Müller Publishers, 2010.

Myers, Marc. "The Man Behind All that Jazz." *The Wall Street Journal*, April 15, 2011.

Nicholson, Stuart. *Jazz-Rock: A History*. Edinburgh, Scotland: Canongate, 1998.

O'Hagan, Sean. "Idol Talk: Joni Mitchell." *New Musical Express*, June 4, 1988. Retrieved March 28, 2024, from http://www.rocksbackpages.com/Library/Article/idol-talk-joni-mitchell

Palmer, Robert. "Survivors in Jazz Rock Disclaim It." *The New York Times*, June 11, 1982, Section C, 22.

Pond, Steven A. *Head Hunters: The Making of Jazz's First Platinum Album*. Ann Arbor, Mich.: University of Michigan Press, 2005.

Rensin, David. "Weather Report: Fair Weather Jazz Fans Leave them Alone." *Rolling Stone*, September 27, 1973. Retrieved from http://www.rocksbackpages.com/Library/Article/weather-report-fair-weather-jazz-fans-leave-them-alone

Russonello, Giovanni. "Chick Corea, Jazz Keyboardist and Innovator, Dies at 79." *The New York Times*, February 12, 2021, Section A, 21.

Santana, Carlos, with Ashley Kahn and Hal Miller. *The Universal Tone: Bringing My Story To Light*. New York: Back Bay Books, 2014.

Shipton, Alyn. *A New History of Jazz*, 2nd ed. New York: Continuum, 2007.

Slaven, Neil. *Electric Don Quixote: The Definitive Story of Frank Zappa*. London: Omnibus Press, 2009.

Snowden, Don. "Jazz Drummer Tony Williams: A Lifetime of Risky Riffs." *Los Angeles Times*, August 17, 1989. Retrieved from https://www.latimes.com/archives/la-xpm-1989-08-17-ca-948-story.html

Stewart, Zan. "The Two Audiences of Freddie Hubbard." *The Los Angeles Times*, January 27, 1988.

Sutcliffe, Phil. "Weather Report: City Hall, Newcastle." *Sounds*, October 14, 1978. Retrieved from http://www.rocksbackpages.com/Library/Article/weather-report-city-hall-newcastle

Sweet, Brian. *Steely Dan: Reelin' in the Years*. London: Omnibus Press, 2015. Kindle.

Swenson, John. "Les McCann: *Layers* (Atlantic)." *Zoo World*, May 9, 1974. Retrieved from http://www.rocksbackpages.com/Library/Article/les-mccann-ilayersi-atlantic

Szwed, John. *So What: The Life of Miles Davis*. New York: Simon & Schuster, 2002.

Taylor, William. "Billy." *The Black Perspective in Music*, 14 (1), Special Issue: Black American Music Symposium 1985 (Winter, 1986): 21–25.

Tingen, Paul. *Miles Beyond: The Electric Explorations of Miles Davis, 1967–1991*. New York: Billboard Books, 2001.

Turner, Pete and Ashley Kahn. *The Color of Jazz: Album Cover Photographs by Pete Turner.* New York: Rizzoli, 2006.

Walls, Richard C. "Weather Report: Mr. Gone (Columbia)." *Creem*, February 1979. Retrieved from http://www.rocksbackpages.com/Library/Article/weather-report-imr-gonei-columbia

Watrous, Peter. "Jazz View: A Jazz Generation and the Miles Davis Curse." *The New York Times*, October 15, 1995, Section 2, 1.

Weber, Eberhard. *Eberhard Weber: A German Jazz Story*, trans. Heidi Kirk. Sheffield: Equinox, 2021.

Welch, Chris. "Mahavishnu Orchestra: Cobham—It Ended in Total Fiasco." *Melody Maker*, February 2, 1974. Retrieved from http://www.rocksbackpages.com/Library/Article/mahavishnu-orchestra-cobham--it-ended-in-total-fiasco

Wenner, Jann. "Blood, Sweat & Tears: Bringing the Brass to Rock and Roll." *Rolling Stone*, April 7, 1968.

West, Hollie I. "Mangione, In Tune with All but the Critics." *The Washington Post*, August 14, 1979.

White, Maurice, with Herb Powell. *My Life With Earth, Wind & Fire.* New York: Amistad, 2016.

Williams, Richard. "Manfred Eicher: The Sound Man." *The Guardian*, July 16, 2010.

Yaffe, David. *Reckless Daughter: A Portrait of Joni Mitchell.* New York: Sarah Crichton Books, 2017.

Yardley, William. "Donald Byrd, Jazz Trumpeter, Dies at 80." *The New York Times*, February 11, 2013, Section A, 28.